Mixed Workouts

The 11+ 10-Minute Tests

For the CEM (Durham University) test

Book 1

Ages
10-11

Practise • Prepare • Pass

Everything your child needs for 11+ success

How to use this book

This book is made up of 10-minute workouts and puzzle pages.
There are answers and detailed explanations in the pull-out section at the back of the book.

10-Minute Workouts

- There are 30 workouts in this book, each containing two different subjects from
  Maths, Verbal Reasoning, Comprehension and Non-Verbal Reasoning.

- Each workout is designed to focus on questions that your child could come across in their
  11+ Test. They cover a variety of skills and techniques at the right difficulty levels.

- If your child hasn't managed to finish the workout in time, they need to work on increasing their
  speed, whereas if they have made a lot of mistakes, they need to work more carefully.

- Keep track of your child's scores using the progress chart on the inside back cover of the book.

Puzzle Pages

- There are 9 puzzle pages in this book, which are a great break from test-style questions.
  They encourage children to practise the same skills that they will need in the test, but in
  a fun way.

Published by CGP

Editors:
Luke Bennett, Tom Carney, Emma Clayton, Emma Cleasby, Alex Fairer, Katherine Faudemer, Sophie Herring,
Hannah Roscoe, Ben Train

With thanks to Will Garrison, Alison Griffin, Sharon Keeley-Holden, David Ryan
and Karen Wells for the proofreading.

Please note that CGP is not associated with CEM or The University of Durham in any way.
This book does not include any official questions and it is not endorsed by CEM or The University of Durham.
CEM, Centre for Evaluation and Monitoring, Durham University and *The University of Durham*
are all trademarks of The University of Durham.

ISBN: 978 1 78294 940 4
Printed by Elanders Ltd, Newcastle upon Tyne
Clipart from Corel®

Based on the classic CGP style created by Richard Parsons.

Contents

Q1-7 will test your **maths** skills.
You have **6 minutes** to complete Q1-7.

1. Yesterday the temperature was 4 °C. Today it is 11 degrees colder.
    What is the temperature today? Circle the correct option.

A	−7 °C	**C**	7 °C	**E**	−6 °C
B	15 °C	**D**	−5 °C		

2. Eduardo puts a cake in the oven at 13:37, for 35 minutes. What time does
    Eduardo take the cake out of the oven? Give your answer in 24-hour clock format.

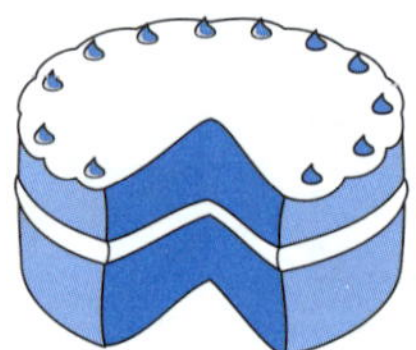

3. The graph below shows a quadrilateral.

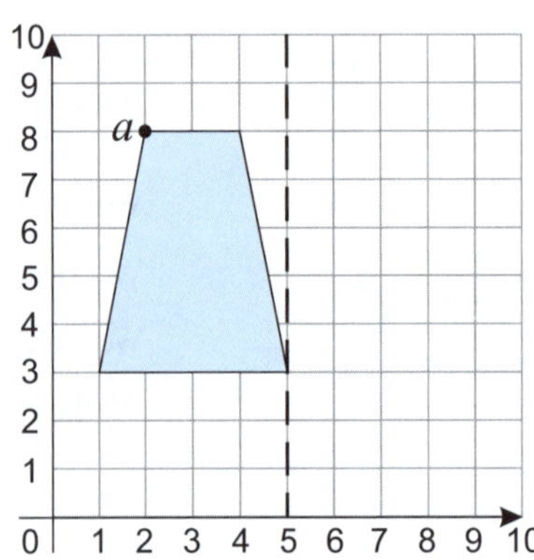

    If the shape is reflected along the dotted line what will the coordinates
    of point *a* of the new reflected shape be?

4. What is the next number in the sequence below? Circle the correct option.

$$^1/_3, \quad 1, \quad 1^2/_3, \quad 2^1/_3$$

A $2^2/_3$ **C** 3   **E** 4

B $3^1/_3$ **D** $3^2/_3$

5. If there are 21 weekdays in April this year, what percentage of April's days
    are weekdays?

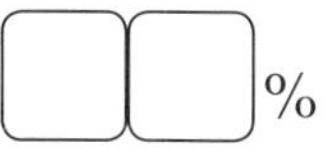
%

6. Franklin has 5 m of ribbon that he uses to wrap 5 small presents
    and 3 large presents. He works out that he needs 50 cm for each small present
    and 80 cm for each large present. How much ribbon will he have left over?

cm

7. A regular hexagon is shown below. *O* is its centre point.

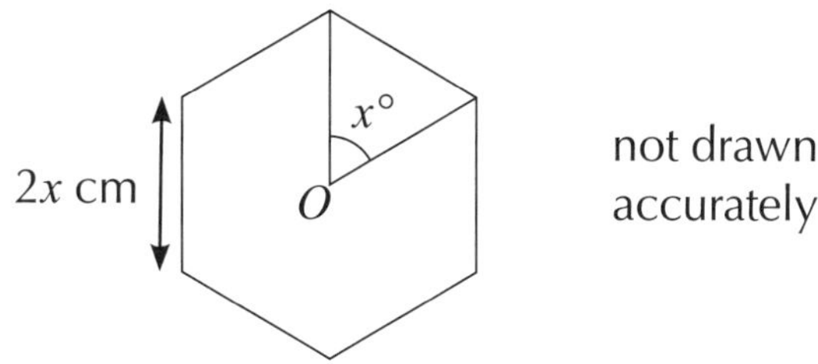

What is the perimeter of the shape? Circle the correct option.

A 5.4 m   **C** 600 cm   **E** 7.2 m

B 3.6 m   **D** 120 cm

Work out which of the options best fits in place of the missing hexagon in the grid.

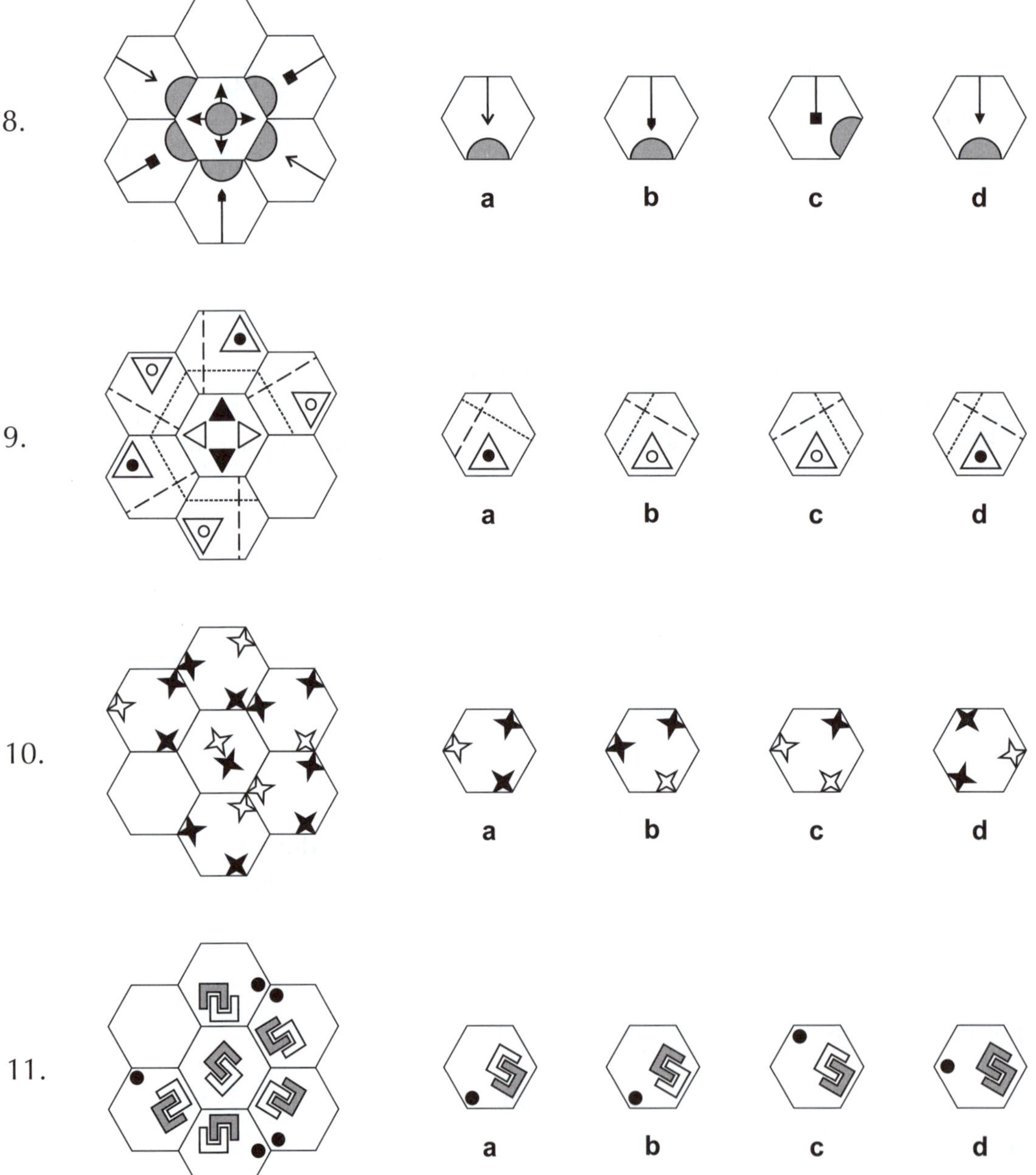

Work out which option is a top-down 2D view of the 3D figure on the left.

12.

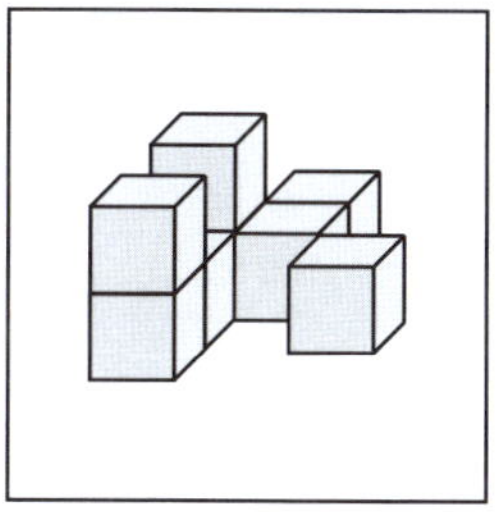

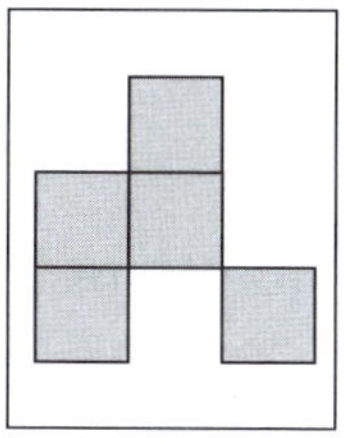

a 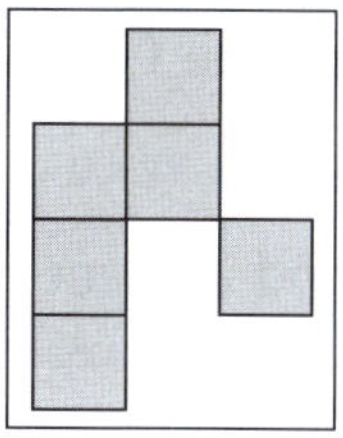   b 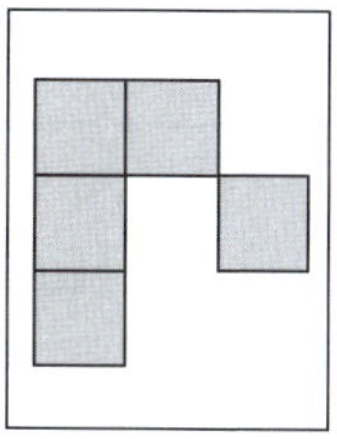   c 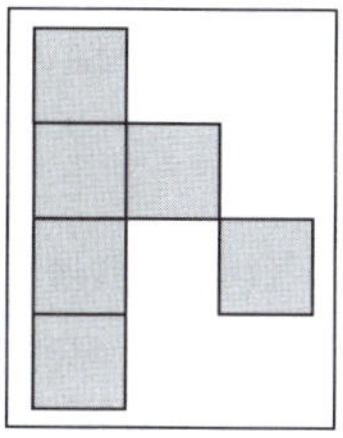   d

13.

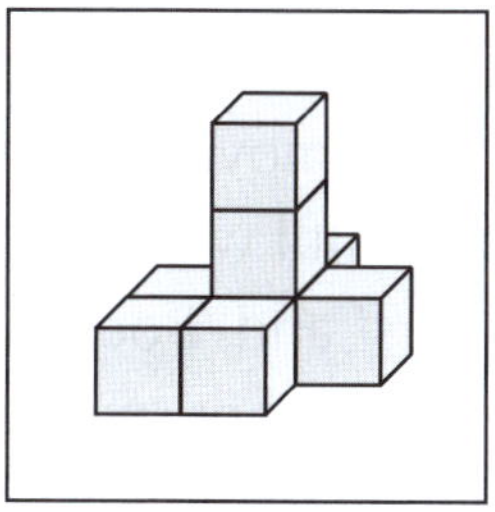

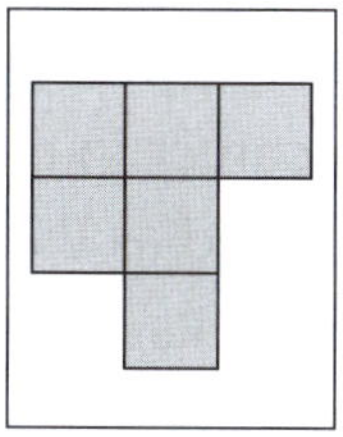

a 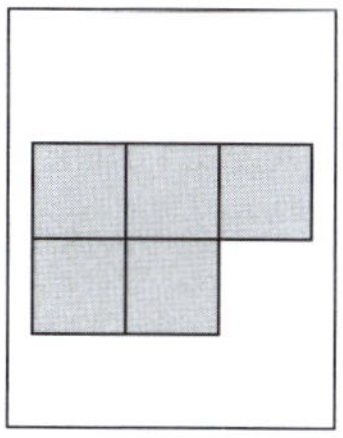   b 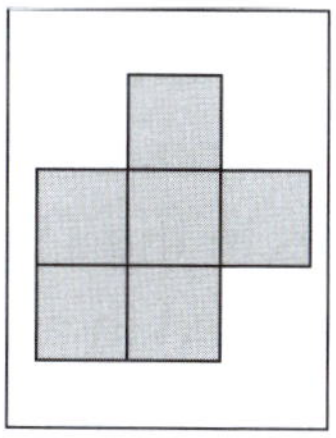   c 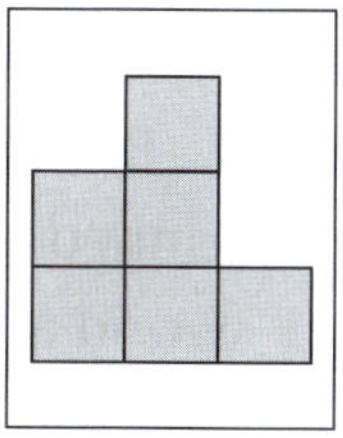   d

14.

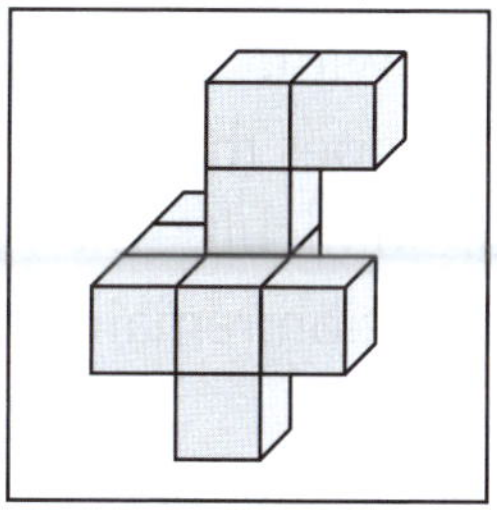

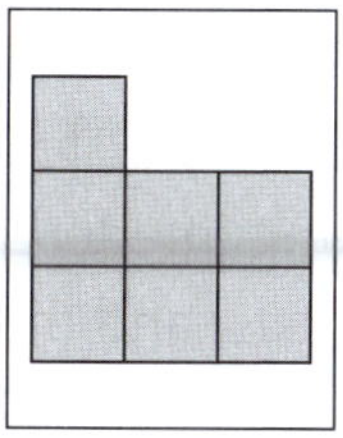

a    b 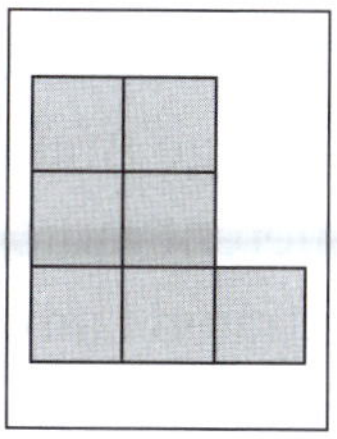   c 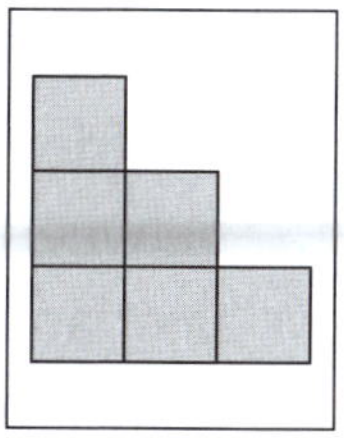   d

/ 14

Q1-7 will test your **comprehension** skills.
You have **6 minutes** to complete Q1-7.

Read this passage carefully and answer the questions that follow.

Hedy Lamarr

During her unusual career, Hedy Lamarr was involved in the glamorous world of
Hollywood films, and she also made significant contributions to science. She became
one of the biggest film stars of her time, as well as inventing a device that paved the
way for Wi-Fi®, Bluetooth® and GPS technology.

5   Born in Vienna, Lamarr began her film career in Europe before moving to the
United States in the 1930s. She was described as the most beautiful woman in the
world and starred in a number of box-office hits, such as 'Algiers' and 'Boom Town'.
She was renowned for her glamour and looks, but few knew that in her spare time she
nurtured an interest in science. Despite a lack of formal scientific training, she studied
10 and became knowledgeable about aviation, aerodynamics and military technology.

    The Second World War spurred Lamarr to use her talents to contribute to the war
effort. She identified a flaw in the US Navy's torpedoes, which were radio-controlled
and could be sent off course if the radio signals were interfered with. Lamarr and
her friend George Antheil designed a guidance system for torpedoes that would 'hop'
15 between different radio frequencies, making interference more difficult. The Navy
later appropriated Lamarr and Antheil's ideas, and their contribution remained
unacknowledged for decades.

    It wasn't until the 1990s that Lamarr and Antheil's work was finally recognised.
Then in her eighties, Lamarr was honoured with awards by the scientific community.
20 Her pioneering work in radio communication is the basis for the wireless transmission
technologies that are so commonly used today.

1. According to the text, which of the following statements about Lamarr must be false?

    A   She had a wide variety of talents.

    B   She worked internationally as an actress.

    C   She invented Bluetooth® technology.

    D   She was well-regarded for her on-screen career.

2. Which of the following best describes what people thought about Lamarr during her film career?

    A   She was considered the best actress of her generation.

    B   She was famed for her beauty.

    C   She was considered eccentric because of her inventions.

    D   She was considered an expert in aviation.

3. According to the text, which of the following statements about Lamarr must be true?

    A   She was an experienced pilot.

    B   She taught herself about science.

    C   She moved to Algiers, Algeria.

    D   She believed beauty was more important than intelligence.

4. What did Lamarr do during the Second World War?

    A   She worked for the US government to help the war effort.

    B   She built torpedoes for the US Navy.

    C   She criticised the war effort.

    D   She worked to improve existing American weaponry.

5. According to the text, what was the problem with the Navy's torpedoes?

    A   They were controlled by weak radio signals.

    B   They interfered with other pieces of equipment.

    C   Enemy forces could send them astray.

    D   They didn't have enough power to get to their destination.

6. Why was Lamarr's work with torpedoes not recognised at first?

   A   The US Navy used Lamarr's work but didn't credit her.

   B   She wanted to be known only for her film career.

   C   No one believed she was capable of inventing anything.

   D   George Antheil got all of the credit.

7. Why was Lamarr given awards in the 1990s?

   A   For inventing many of today's wireless technologies.

   B   For continuing to make inventions well into her eighties.

   C   For her work in radio communication technology.

   D   For her contribution to the film industry.

Q8-12 will test your **maths** skills.
You have **4 minutes** to complete Q8-12.

8. How many lines of symmetry does the following shape have?
Circle the correct option.

A	0	**C**	2	**E**	8
B	1	**D**	4		

8

9.   What is $6^2 \times (72 - 68)$?

10. Work out the area of the shape below.

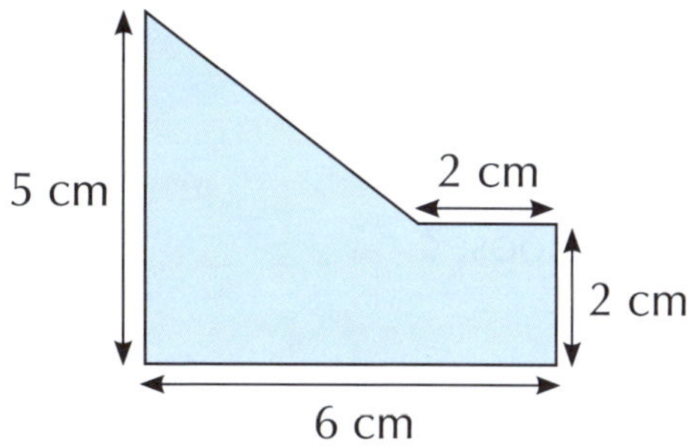

 cm²

Look at the diagram below.

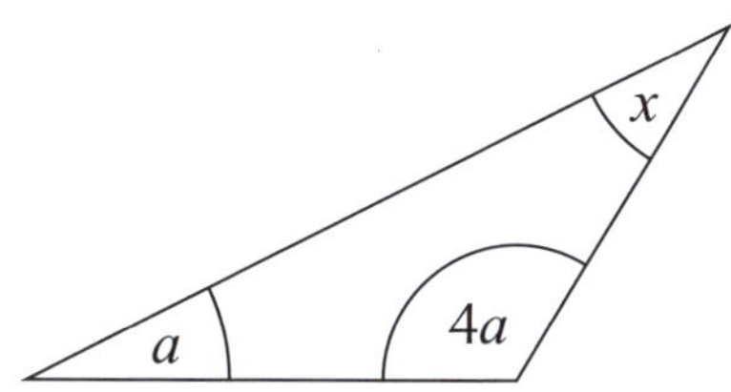

11   Which of the following equations is correct? Circle the correct option.

    A $x = 2a - 180$ **C** $x = 180 - 5a$ **E** $x + 4a = 180$

    B $90 - 4a = a$ **D** $4a = 270$

12. If $a = 30°$, what is the value of x?

    °

/ 12

Workout 2

These puzzles are a great way to practise your **matching** and **word-unscrambling** skills.

Alien Antics

Garry the alien is working undercover on Planet Zog. He needs a disguise that will make him look as similar as possible to the local aliens. Which outfit should he choose?

Local aliens

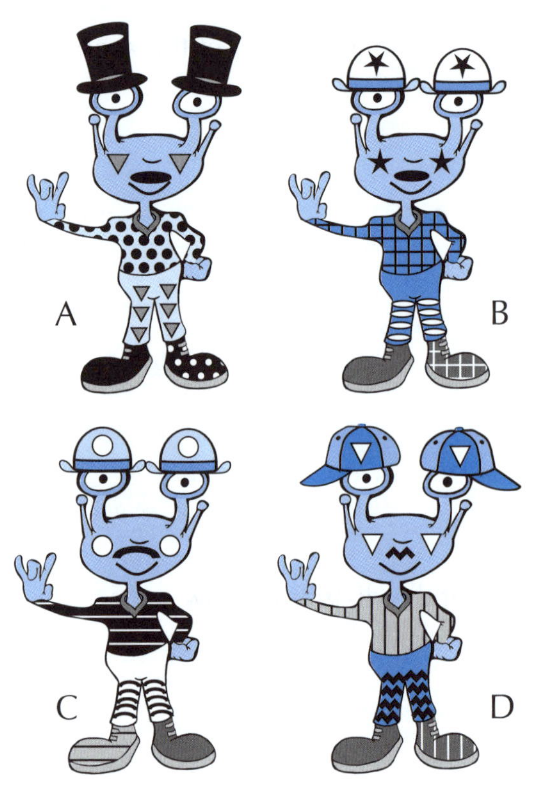

Cooking Crisis

Paula is making a three-course meal, but she's forgotten some of the ingredients. Unscramble the anagrams below to work out what the forgotten ingredients are. The name of a final ingredient is also hidden in the words below. Unscramble the highlighted letters to work out what it is.

SNIRPAPS

MOOTATES

SARCUTD

ROGANES

GILCAR

CIBUISST

The final ingredient is ___________ .

Q1-11 will test your **non-verbal reasoning** skills.
You have **6 minutes** to complete Q1-11.

Look at how the first two figures are changed, and then work out which option would look like the third figure if you changed it in the same way.

1.

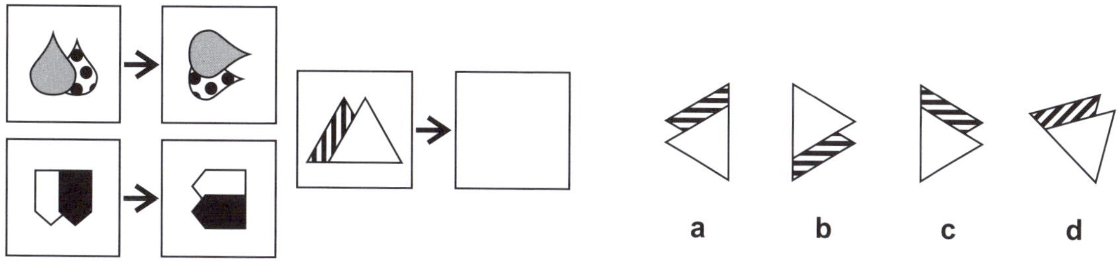

    a   b   c   d

2.

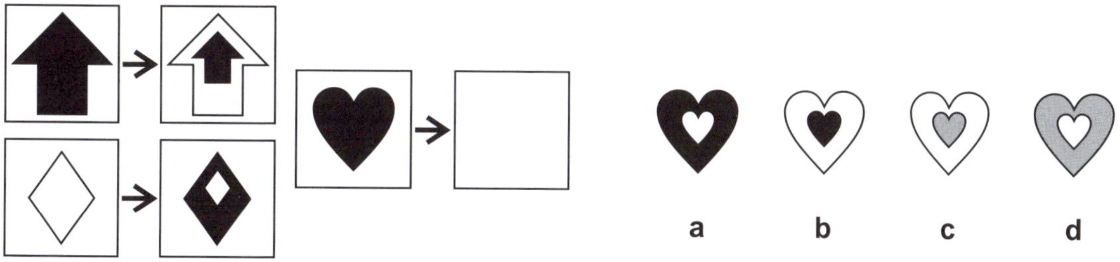

    a   b   c   d

3.

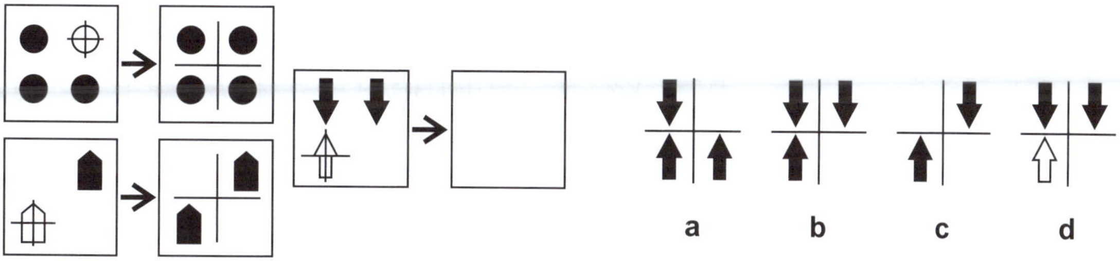

    a   b   c   d

4.

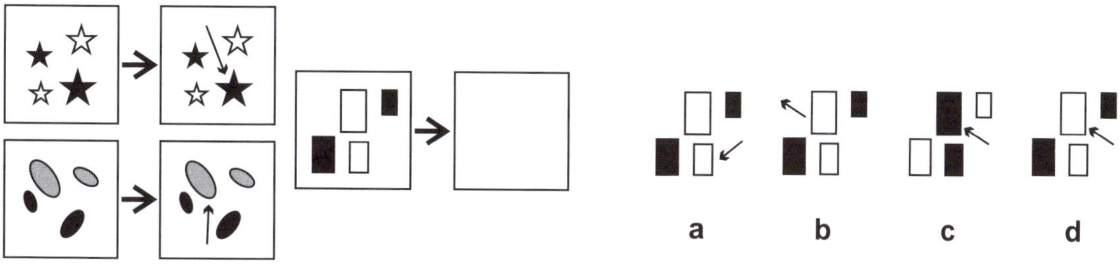

    a   b   c   d

Work out which of the four cubes can be made from the net.

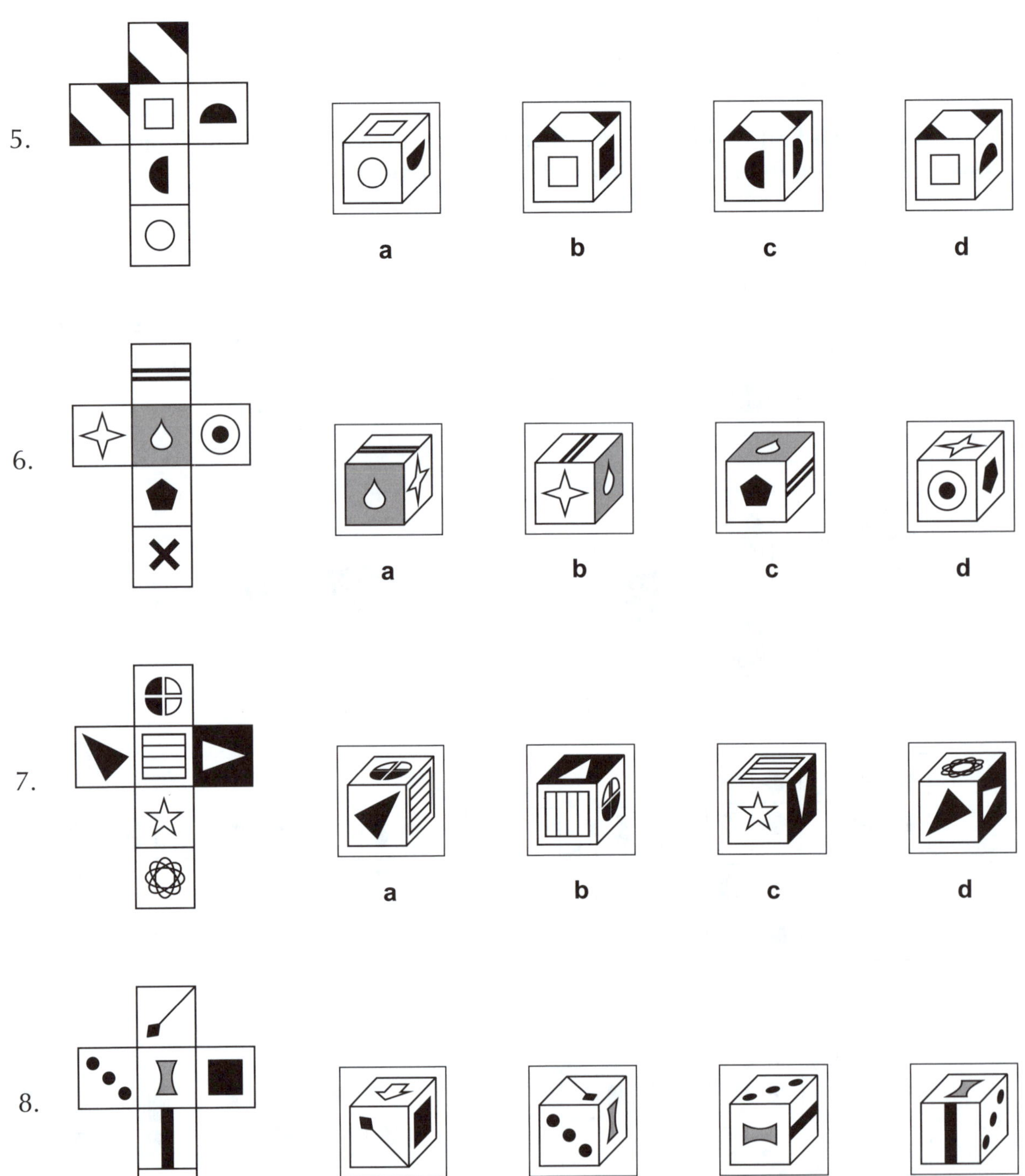

9.

  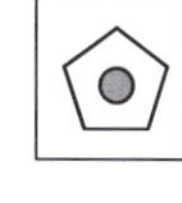  

a   b   c   d   e

10.

a   b   c   d   e

11.

a   b   c   d   e

In each question below, the words can be rearranged to form a sentence.
One word doesn't fit in the sentence. Underline the word that doesn't fit.

Example: red   the   has   <u>ride</u>   girl   bicycle   a

12. obtain   licence   before   a   in   must   you   to   cars   drive   order

13. storm   went   got   and   exercise   a   in   caught   out   walking   we

14. working   arrived   several   fix   bathroom   to   plumbers   flooded   the

15. wearing   red   ball   not   did   Chuckles   his   nose   clown   the   like

16. sheep   a   fence   slip   in   allowed   my   escape   to   hole   three

17. in   carrots   eating   helps   the   dark   to   vision   you   see

Find the word that means the opposite, or nearly the opposite,
of the word on the left.

Example: **first**   later   <u>last</u>   next   beginning

18. **arid**   moist   sharp   frosty   misty

19. **calm**   dormant   acrid   flustered   sullen

20. **increase**   languish   wane   dim   slacken

21. **honesty**   stealth   slander   betrayal   deceit

22. **depression**   relief   euphoria   frenzy   keenness

23. **selfish**   amiable   pompous   tolerant   altruistic

/ 23

Q1-11 will test your **non-verbal reasoning** skills.
You have **6 minutes** to complete Q1-11.

Work out which option would look like the figure on the left if it was rotated.

Rotate

1.     

a   b   c   d

Rotate

2.     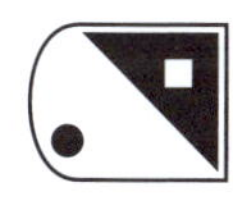

a   b   c   d

Rotate

3.     

a   b   c   d

Rotate

4.     

a   b   c   d

Rotate

5. 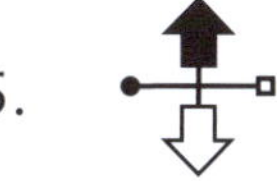  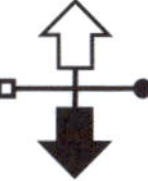  

a   b   c   d

Work out which option is most like the two figures on the left.

6.

7.

8.

9.

10.

11.

12. The population of a town is 56 713. Round the population to the nearest thousand.

13. Next year 2824 people will move out of the town. What will the population of the town be after the people leave?

14. The nth term of a sequence is $3(n + 5)$. What is the 18th term of the sequence?

A   59   **C**   33   **E**   26

B   72   **D**   69

15. A shop sells 4 different colours of pencil case. The pie chart shows how many pencil cases of each colour were sold last month. They sold 216 pencil cases in total.

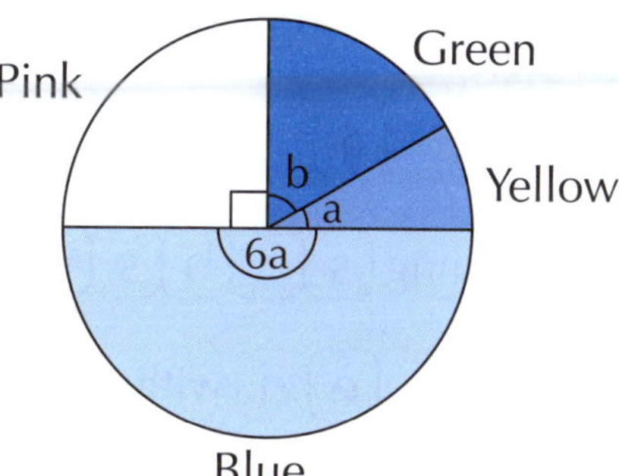

Half the pencil cases sold were blue. How many green pencil cases were sold?

/ 15

Workout 5

Q1-10 will test your **verbal reasoning** skills.
You have **4 minutes** to complete Q1-10.

Fill in the missing letters to complete the words in the following passage.

1. The city of Venice is renowned for its ⬚ t ⬚ ⬚ ⬚ d i ⬚ i ⬚ ⬚ n of masks.

2. Popular with today's tourists as ⬚ ⬚ u v ⬚ n i ⬚ s, they are widely

3. a ⬚ ⬚ o c ⬚ ⬚ t e d with the Carnival of Venice — this annual

4. festival provides an ⬚ p p ⬚ ⬚ ⬚ u ⬚ ⬚ t y for revellers to dress up

5. and disguise themselves. Some masks are ⬚ r n ⬚ t ⬚ l ⬚ decorated

6. with jewels and feathers, while others are a ⬚ t a ⬚ k white. Some conceal

    the wearer's whole face, while others only cover the eyes. One of the most iconic

7. masks is the ⬚ i n ⬚ s t ⬚ r *Medico della peste*, which has a long,

    curved beak. This mask wasn't originally a part of the carnival celebrations,

8. but rather a protective m ⬚ a ⬚ u ⬚ e taken by plague doctors in the

9. 17th century. Sweet-smelling s ⬚ b s ⬚ ⬚ n c ⬚ ⬚ such as flowers

10. were ⬚ o ⬚ t a ⬚ n e d within the beak, as at the time it was believed

    that foul smells were responsible for spreading infection.

18

Work out which of the options best fits in place of the missing hexagon in the grid.

11.

12.

13.

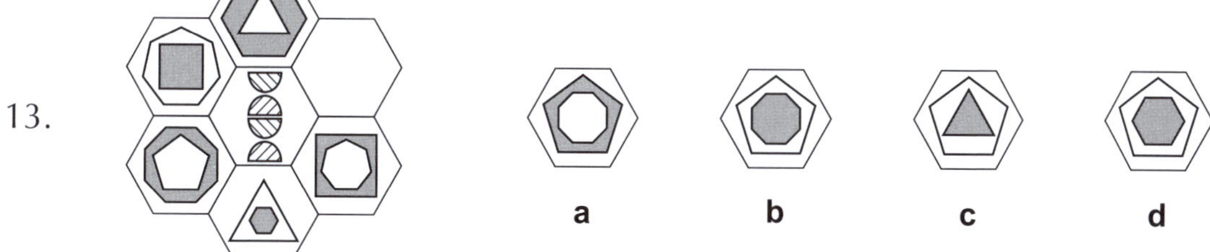

Look at how the first two figures are changed, and then work out which option would look like the third figure if you changed it in the same way.

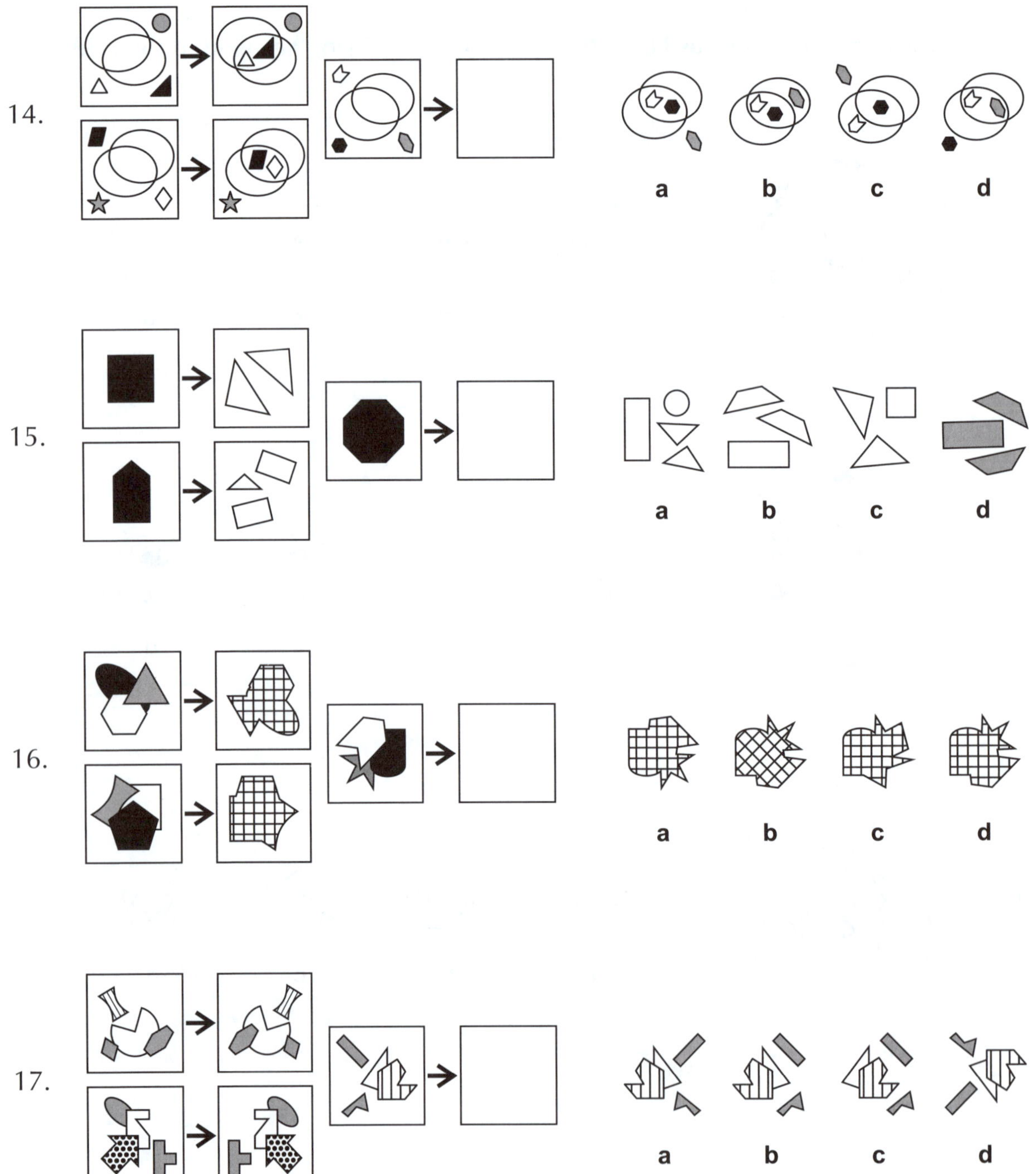

14.
a   b   c   d

15.
a   b   c   d

16.
a   b   c   d

17.
a   b   c   d

18.

a   b   c   d

19.

a   b   c   d

20.

a   b   c   d

21.

a   b   c   d

/ 21

21

Workout 5

These puzzles are a fun way to practise with **prime numbers** and **3D views**.

Prime Ribs

A medieval theme restaurant has long tables and benches instead of chairs. The restaurant only has benches that can seat a prime number of people and no bench can seat more than 10 people. But the staff say they can use their benches to seat groups of customers of any size without leaving any spaces on the benches.

- What is the smallest number of benches that can be used to seat a group of 11, without leaving any empty spaces?

- How about a group of 18?

- What's the smallest group size that would need more than four benches?

Jungle Jump!

Otto is parachuting into the dense Blockadia jungle when he see five mysterious piles of blocks.

From above, the dark blue blocks spell out a word.

What is the secret word?

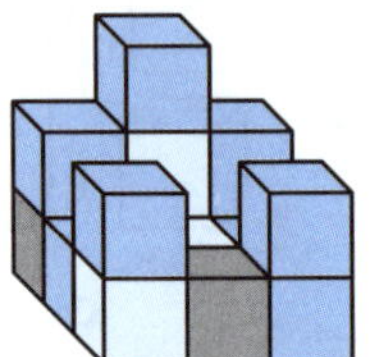 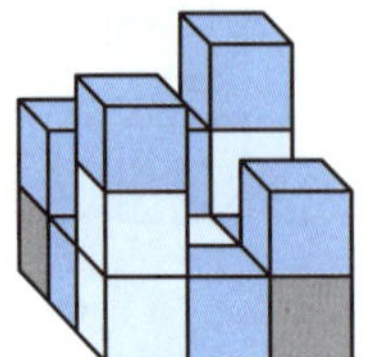 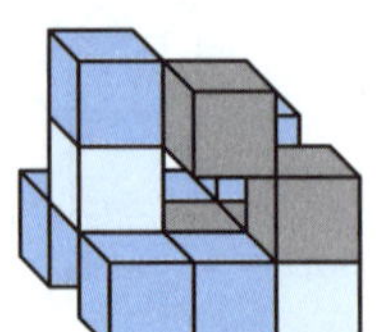  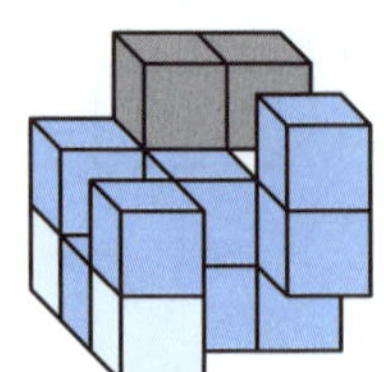

Workout 6

Q1-5 will test your **maths** skills.
You have **4 minutes** to complete Q1-5.

Below is part of a timetable for the X2 bus.

Stop	Hallow	Wilt	Clawson	Bardgrove
Time	11:54	12:27	12:46	13:08

1. How long does the bus take to get from Hallow to Bardgrove?

 minutes

2. Give the shortest time the bus travels between two stops. Circle the correct option.

A 22 minutes **C** 13 minutes **E** 33 minutes

B 9 minutes **D** 19 minutes

3. One week Ruben earns £240. He spends 20% of the money on bike accessories. How much does Ruben have left? Circle the correct option.

A £200 **C** £172 **E** £168

B £192 **D** £180

4. The volume of the cuboid below is 144 cm³. What is the height of the cuboid?

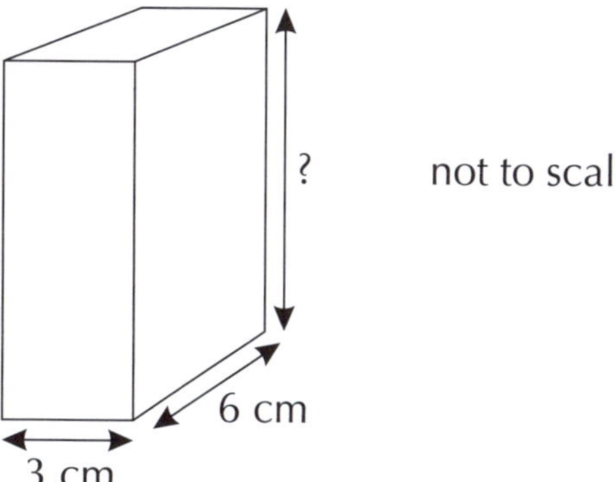

cm

5. Alessandro recorded the number of cars that passed his house everyday between 1 pm and 2 pm in a bar chart.

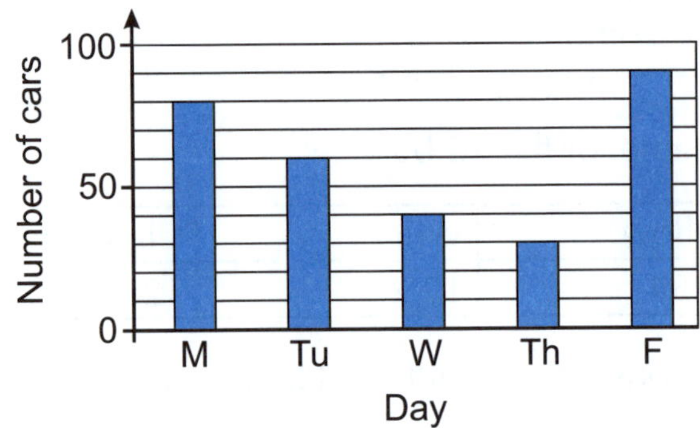

Work out the mean number of cars that passed Alessandro's house every minute during the time he was recording.

Q6-23 will test your **verbal reasoning** skills.
You have **6 minutes** to complete Q6-23.

Three of the words in each list are linked. Mark the word that is not related to these three.

Example: journal   diary   <u>textbook</u>   notebook

6.   glow   bright   glare   shine

7.   hammer   mallet   beat   pound

8.   report   fax   text   email

9.   drain   milk   water   bleed

10. feline   bovine   canine   alpine

24

Mark the word outside the brackets that has a similar meaning to the words in both sets of brackets.

Example: (twig   branch)   (fasten   attach)   glue   <u>stick</u>   affix   bough

11. (trail   way)   (shadow   stalk)   seek   capture   tail   track

12. (dismal   gloomy)   (evil   black)   dim   sinful   dark   unlit

13. (convoy   caravan)   (school   educate)   train   practice   retinue   drill

14. (decelerate   brake)   (leisurely   unhurried)   lagged   creep   slow   suspend

15. (realise   recognise)   (value   prize)   fathom   espy   appreciate   extol

16. (dear   intimate)   (finish   end)   close   goal   expire   fast

Complete the word on the right so that it means the same, or nearly the same, as the word on the left.

Example: scared   a f r a i d

17. unexciting   m _ n _ _ n e

18. question   i _ t e _ r o _ a _ e

19. thankfulness   _ r a _ i t _ _ e

20. dismissal   _ _ _ j e _ t i _ n

21. determined   r _ s _ l u _ e

22. indispensable   e _ s _ n _ i a _

23. satisfactory   _ d _ q _ _ t e

/ 23

Workout 6

Q1-7 will test your **comprehension** skills.
You have **6 minutes** to complete Q1-7.

Read this passage carefully and answer the questions that follow.

An adapted extract from 'Moby Dick'

I had not been seated very long ere* a man of a certain venerable robustness entered; immediately as the storm-pelted door flew back upon admitting him, a quick regardful eyeing of him by all the congregation, sufficiently attested that this fine old man was the chaplain**. Yes, it was the famous Father Mapple, so called by
5   the whalemen, among whom he was a very great favourite. He had been a sailor and a harpooneer*** in his youth, but for many years past had dedicated his life to the Church. When he entered I observed that he carried no umbrella, and certainly had not come in his carriage, for his tarpaulin hat ran down with melting sleet, and his great pilot cloth jacket seemed almost to drag him to the floor with the weight of
10 the water it had absorbed. However, hat and coat and overshoes were one by one removed, and hung up in a little space in an adjacent corner; when, arrayed in a decent suit, he quietly approached the pulpit.

Like most old fashioned pulpits, it was a very lofty one, and since a regular stairs to such a height would seriously contract the already small area of the chapel, the
15 architect, it seemed, had acted upon the hint of Father Mapple, and finished the pulpit without a stairs, substituting a perpendicular side ladder, like those used in mounting a ship from a boat at sea. Halting for an instant at the foot of the ladder, Father Mapple cast a look upwards, and then with a truly sailor-like but still reverential dexterity, hand over hand, mounted the steps as if ascending the main-top**** of his vessel.

Hermann Melville

* ere — *before*

** chaplain — *minister of religion*

*** harpooneer — *someone who uses a harpoon (a type of spear)*

**** main-top — *platform on a ship's mainmast*

1. Which of the following best describes the state of the chapel door in line 2?

   A   It has been destroyed by the storm.

   B   It has been soaked by rain from the storm.

   C   It has been blown open by the storm.

   D   It has a special coating on it to protect it from the storm.

2. How does the narrator quickly determine that the old man entering the chapel is Father Mapple?

   A   The narrator has met Father Mapple before.

   B   The old man is dressed like a chaplain.

   C   He notices that the congregation respect the old man.

   D   The members of the congregation greet Father Mapple by name.

3. Which of the following statements about Father Mapple is true?

   A   He has only recently become a chaplain.

   B   He has been a chaplain for a long time.

   C   He is still a sailor.

   D   He has recently retired from working as a sailor.

4. Why does the narrator believe that Father Mapple didn't come to the chapel in a carriage?

   A   He notices that Father Mapple has an umbrella.

   B   He knows that Father Mapple doesn't own a carriage.

   C   He sees that Father Mapple's clothes are completely drenched.

   D   He realises that Father Mapple's shoes are covered in mud.

5. What does the word "lofty" (line 13) mean?

   A   Elevated   **C**   Modest

   B   Opulent   **D**   Spacious

6. Why does the pulpit have a ladder rather than stairs?

    A   The architect thought it would look better.

    B   Stairs were too expensive to build.

    C   All old-fashioned pulpits have ladders.

    D   A ladder takes up less space than stairs.

7. Which of the following best describes Father Mapple as he climbs up the pulpit?

    A   Nimble and dignified

    B   Speedy and boisterous

    C   Slow and laboured

    D   Apprehensive and serious

> Q8-14 will test your **non-verbal reasoning** skills.
> You have **4 minutes** to complete Q8-14.

Work out which of the options best fits in place of the missing square in the series.

8.

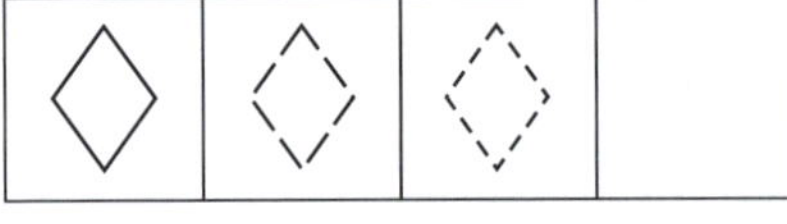

   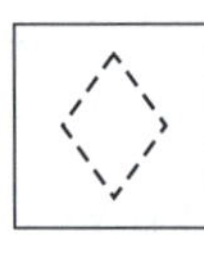   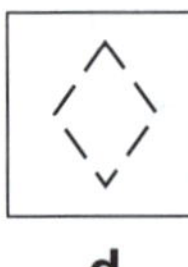

    a   b   c   d

9.

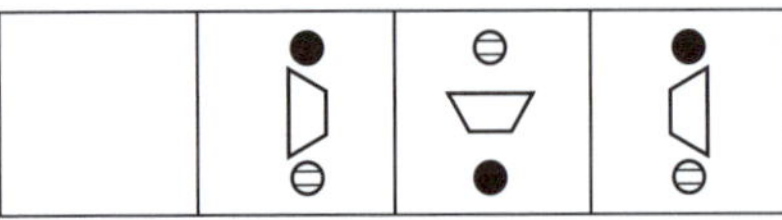

    a   b   c   d

10.

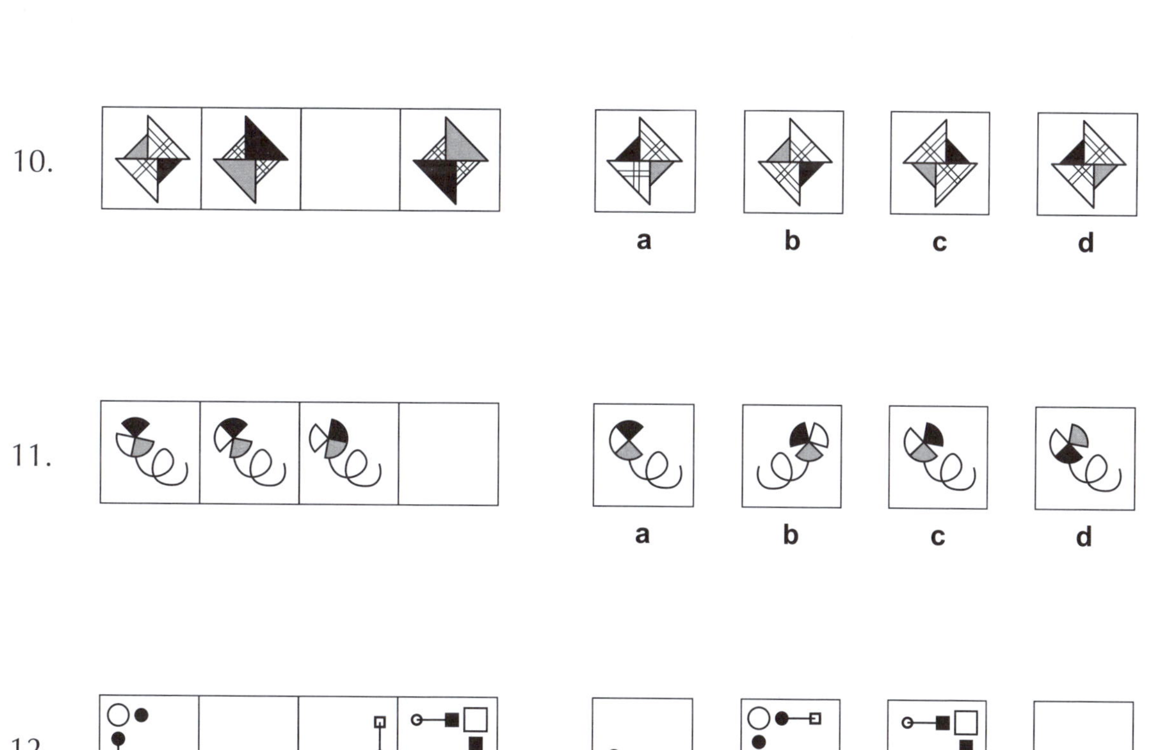

    a   **b**   **c**   **d**

11.

    a   **b**   **c**   **d**

12.

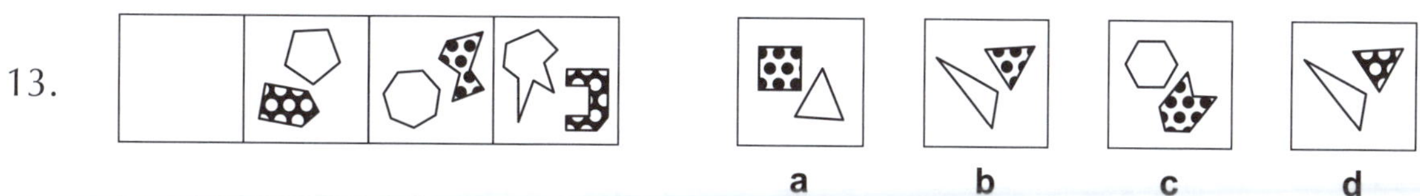

    a   **b**   **c**   **d**

13.

    a   **b**   **c**   **d**

14.

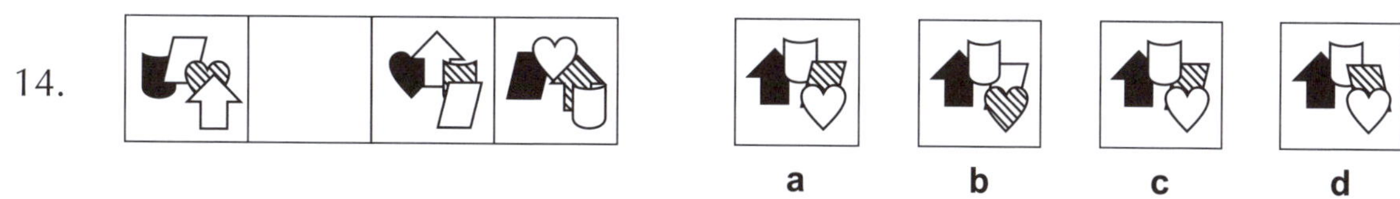

    a   **b**   **c**   **d**

/ 14

Workout 7

Q1-5 will test your **maths** skills.
You have **4 minutes** to complete Q1-5.

1. Which of the following nets makes a pentagonal prism? Circle the correct option.

A 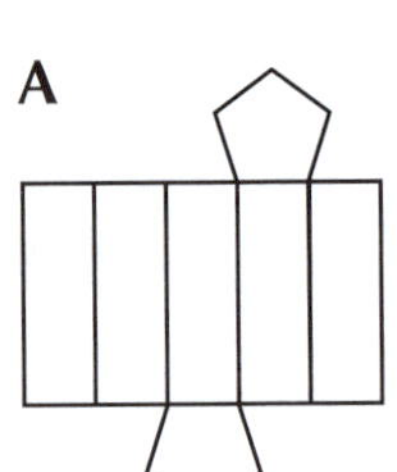 **B** 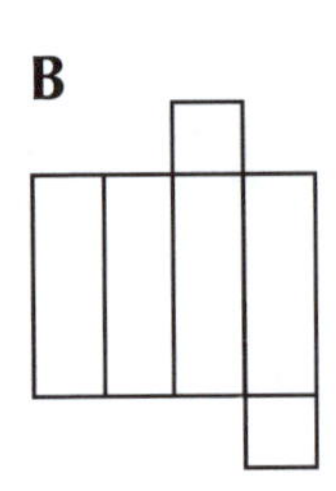 **C** 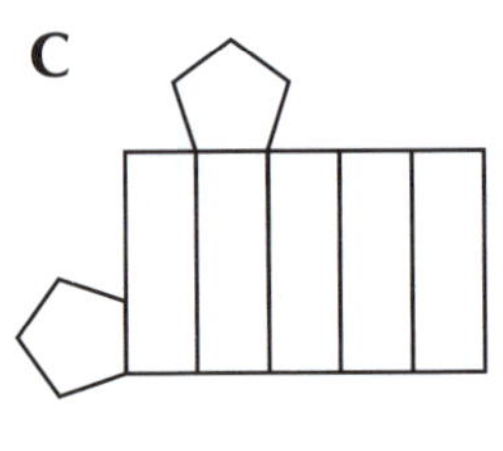 **D** 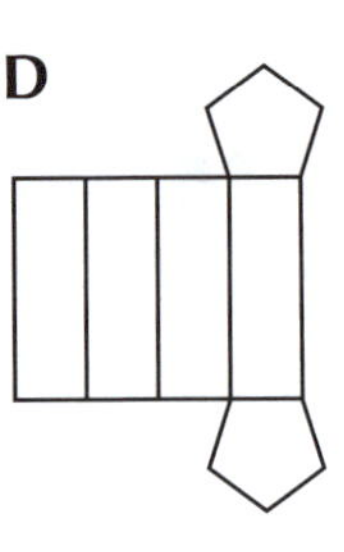 **E** 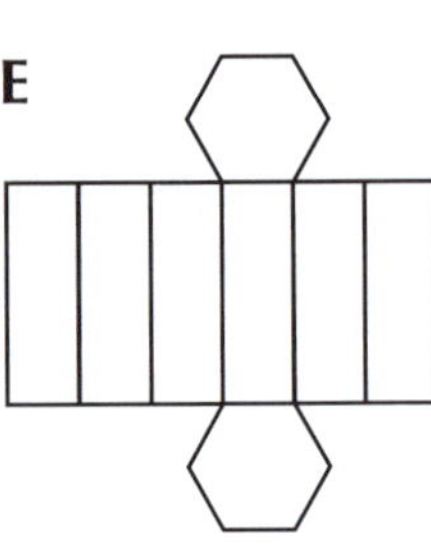

The heights of five sunflowers in Yvonne's garden are:

120 cm, 0.9 m, 1.15 m, 1.85 m, 90 cm

2. What is the difference between the 2nd tallest and 3rd tallest sunflower?

cm

3. Work out the mean height of Yvonne's sunflowers.

m

Rohima is running in a 3.5 km race. She is 780 m from the finishing line.

4. How far has Rohima run so far? Circle the correct option.

    A 2.2 km   **C** 2.68 km   **E** 2.84 km
    B 2.52 km   **D** 2.72 km

5. Rohima jogs the last 780 m to the finish line, at a speed of 4 m per second.
   How long will it take her to reach the finish line?

minutes   seconds

Q6-16 will test your **non-verbal reasoning** skills.
You have **6 minutes** to complete Q6-16.

Work out which 3D figure in the grey box has been rotated to make the new 3D figure.

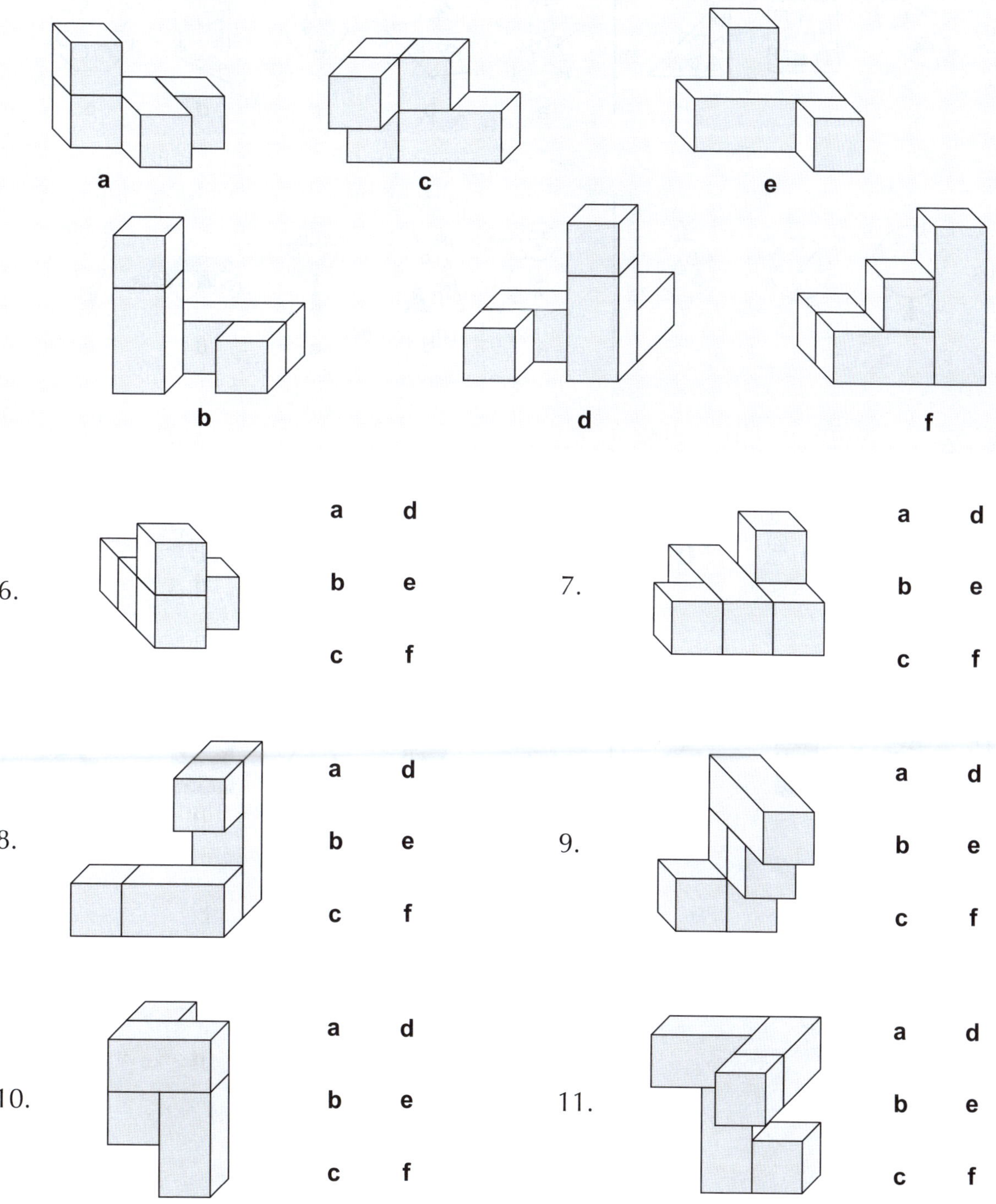

a

c

e

b

d

f

6.

a	d
b	e
c	f

7.

a	d
b	e
c	f

8.

a	d
b	e
c	f

9.

a	d
b	e
c	f

10.

a	d
b	e
c	f

11.

a	d
b	e
c	f

Workout 8

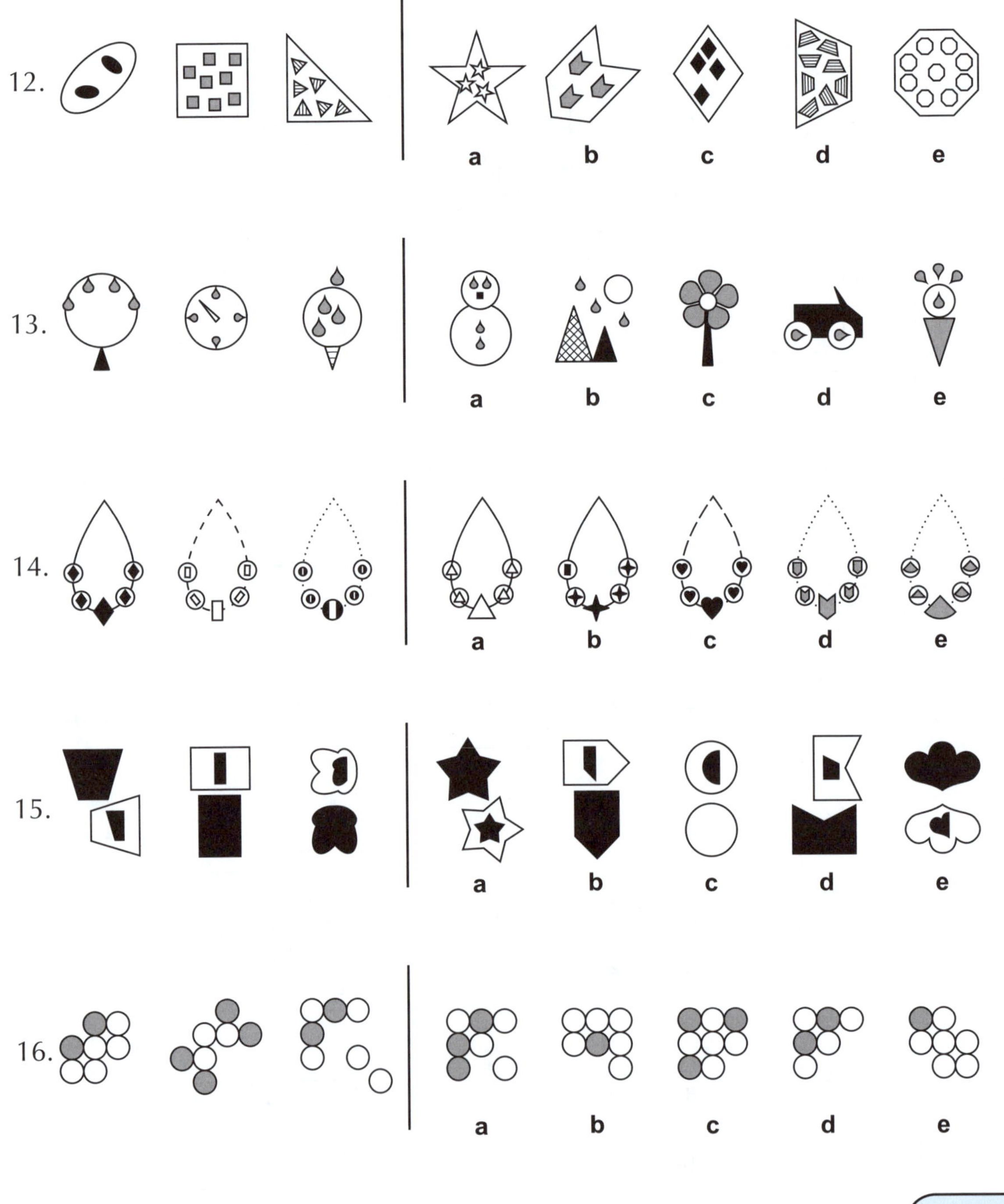

12.
13.
14.
15.
16.

/ 16

Have a go at these puzzles for a fun way to practise **maths reasoning** and **antonyms**.

Scaly Surprise

Harriet works in a zoo. A crocodile egg has been accidentally mixed up with five penguin eggs. Harriet needs to find which is the crocodile egg before it hatches. She can't tell by looking but she knows all the penguin eggs weigh exactly the same and the crocodile egg is a little bit heavier. She decides to use balance scales to find the crocodile egg.

What is the fewest number of times Harriet needs to use the scales to be sure of finding the crocodile egg?

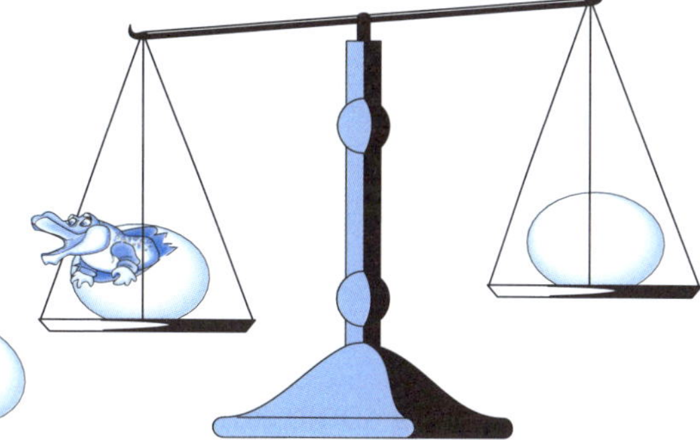

Antonym Actions

Complete the wordsearch by finding an **antonym** for each of the verbs below. Write each antonym on the correct line. The first letter of each antonym has been done for you.

resist   s___________

divide   c___________

continue   q___________

facilitate o___________

expand   s___________

clean   s___________

heed   i___________

E	S	H	R	I	N	K	T	I	B
H	L	O	P	T	Q	C	M	W	A
S	A	H	I	D	U	S	H	K	E
T	S	U	R	R	E	N	D	E	R
A	Q	D	T	A	V	F	R	C	O
I	O	S	Y	E	G	I	R	J	N
N	B	E	N	I	B	M	O	C	G
O	G	A	X	K	L	S	P	D	I

Q1-8 will test your **maths** skills.
You have **6 minutes** to complete Q1-8.

1. The ages of children in an activity club are: 6, 7, 6, 5, 8, 6, 7, 7, 8, 4, 5, 7.
   What is the most common age in the club?

2. What is $^1/_4 + {}^3/_8$? Circle the correct option.

   A $^5/_8$ **C** $^4/_{32}$ **E** $^1/_2$

   B $^2/_8$ **D** $^4/_4$

3. Amber is doing some athletics training. She trains by sprinting 115 m and then
   resting before sprinting again. She sprints 7 times. How far does she run in total?
   Circle the correct option.

   A 735 m   **C** 775 m   **E** 480 m

   B 625 m   **D** 805 m

4. Two regular pentagons are shown in the
   diagram below. What is the value of x?

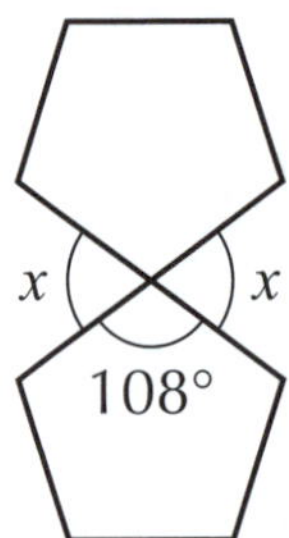

5. If $y = 52 \div 13$, what is y^3? Circle the correct option.

A	64	**C**	124	**E**	48
B	27	**D**	16		

The pictogram shows the number of cars that started and finished three motor races.

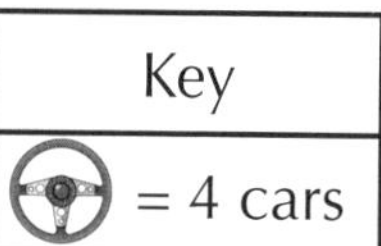

Race 1	Started	(wheels)
	Finished	(wheels)
Race 2	Started	(wheels)
	Finished	(wheels)
Race 3	Started	(wheels)
	Finished	(wheels)

6. What is the mean number of cars that started the three races?

7. What percentage of the cars that started Race 2 finished it?

%

8. A triangle with an 8 cm base had a smaller triangle cut off one corner.
    The new shape now has a 6 cm base and is shown below.
    Work out the area of the new shape.

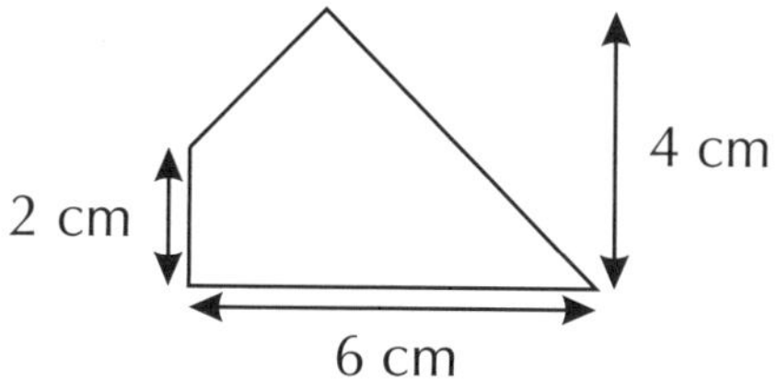

cm²

35

Find the word that means the same, or nearly the same, as the word on the left.

Example: **wide**   flat   straight   <u>broad</u>   long

9. **flourish**   complete   gain   glorify   burgeon

10. **sustenance**   vigour   nourishment   ingestion   supplement

11. **detached**   aloof   prejudiced   ignorant   oblivious

12. **target**   quarry   total   harassment   allocation

13. **subsequently**   subjectively   afterwards   erstwhile   ensuing

14. **ransack**   pillage   explore   accuse   rummage

Complete the word on the right so that it means the opposite, or nearly the opposite, of the word on the left.

Example: heavy   l i g h t

15. agitated   s _ _ r _ _ e

16. affluence   _ o _ e r _ y

17. replenished   e _ _ a _ s t _ d

18. heedfully   _ a _ e _ e _ s l y

19. organised   h _ p _ a z _ r d

/ 19

Q1-10 will test your **verbal reasoning** skills.
You have **4 minutes** to complete Q1-10.

Choose the correct words to complete the passage below.

It is incredible to think that over 65 million years ago, dinosaurs

1. ☐ stalk
   ☐ maundered
   ☐ roamed
   ☐ pursued

Earth.

Today, paleontologists (scientists who

2. ☐ explore
   ☐ critique
   ☐ study
   ☐ scrutiny

dinosaurs), have a wealth of

3. ☐ displaying
   ☐ buried
   ☐ interred
   ☐ excavated

fossils at their disposal to assist them in learning more about these

magnificent ancient reptiles. A

4. ☐ immediate
   ☐ perennial
   ☐ sobering
   ☐ especial

favourite amongst many dinosaur

5. ☐ operators
   ☐ participants
   ☐ detractors
   ☐ enthusiasts

is the Triceratops, with its

6. ☐ iconic
   ☐ uniquely
   ☐ draconic
   ☐ rarity

horns and a large

protective shield on its head. This dinosaur has been frequently portrayed

7. ☐ to
   ☐ in
   ☐ on
   ☐ onto

films and television programmes, making it an immediately recognisable remnant of

8. ☐ Accordingly
☐ Contrary
☐ Similarly
☐ Incompatible

the distant past.   to what you might expect, dinosaurs' closest

living relatives on the planet today are birds. In fact, chickens are thought to be

9. ☐ progeniture   10. ☐ frenetic
☐ linked   ☐ menace
☐ descendants of the ☐ terrorise   Tyrannosaurus Rex — information worth
☐ relative   ☐ formidable

bearing in mind the next time you are about to call someone 'chicken'!

> Q11-21 will test your **non-verbal reasoning** skills.
> You have **6 minutes** to complete Q11-21.

Find the figure in each row that is most unlike the others.

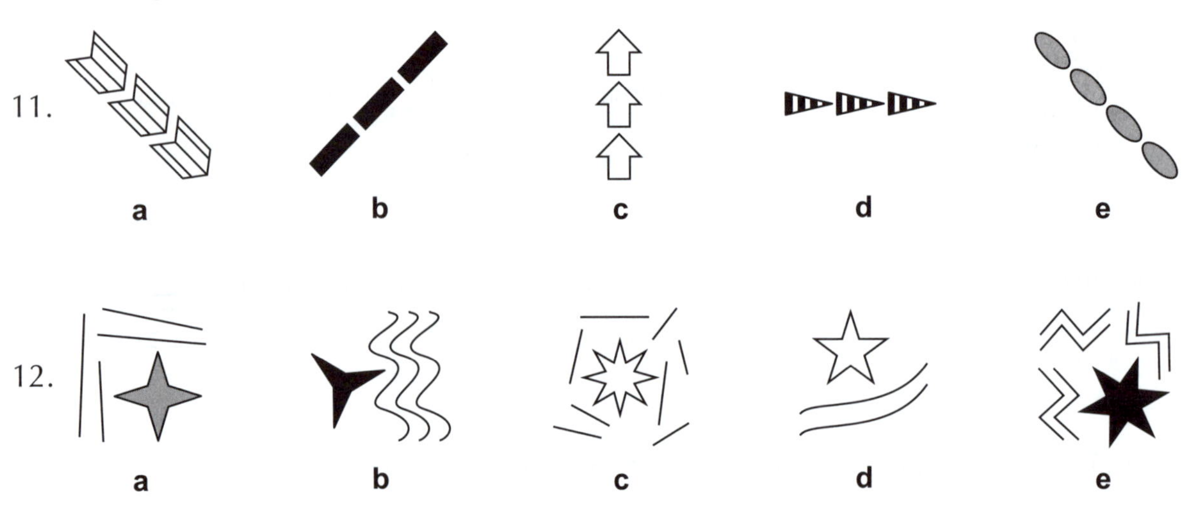

13. 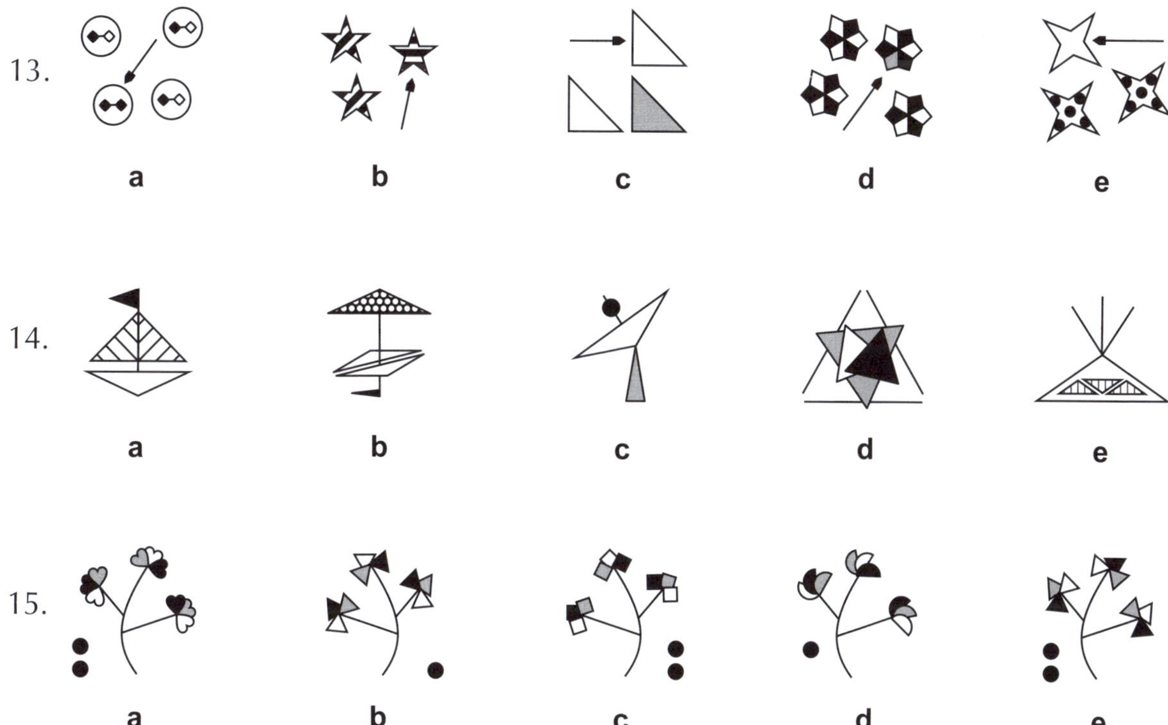

14.

15.

Work out which of the options best fits in place of the missing square in the grid.

16.

17.

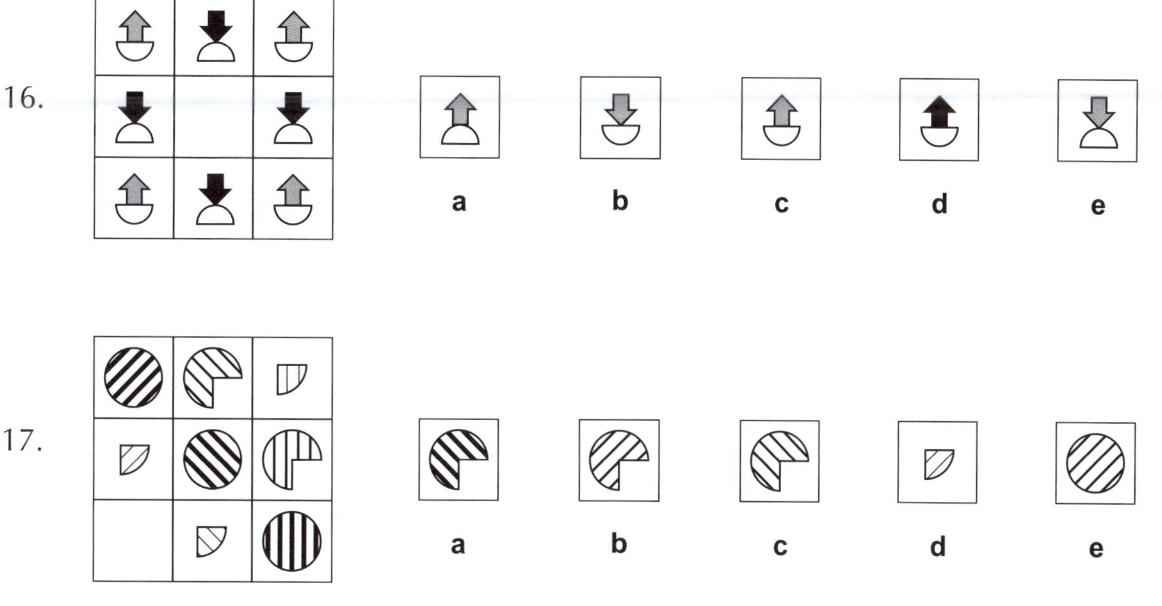

Workout 10

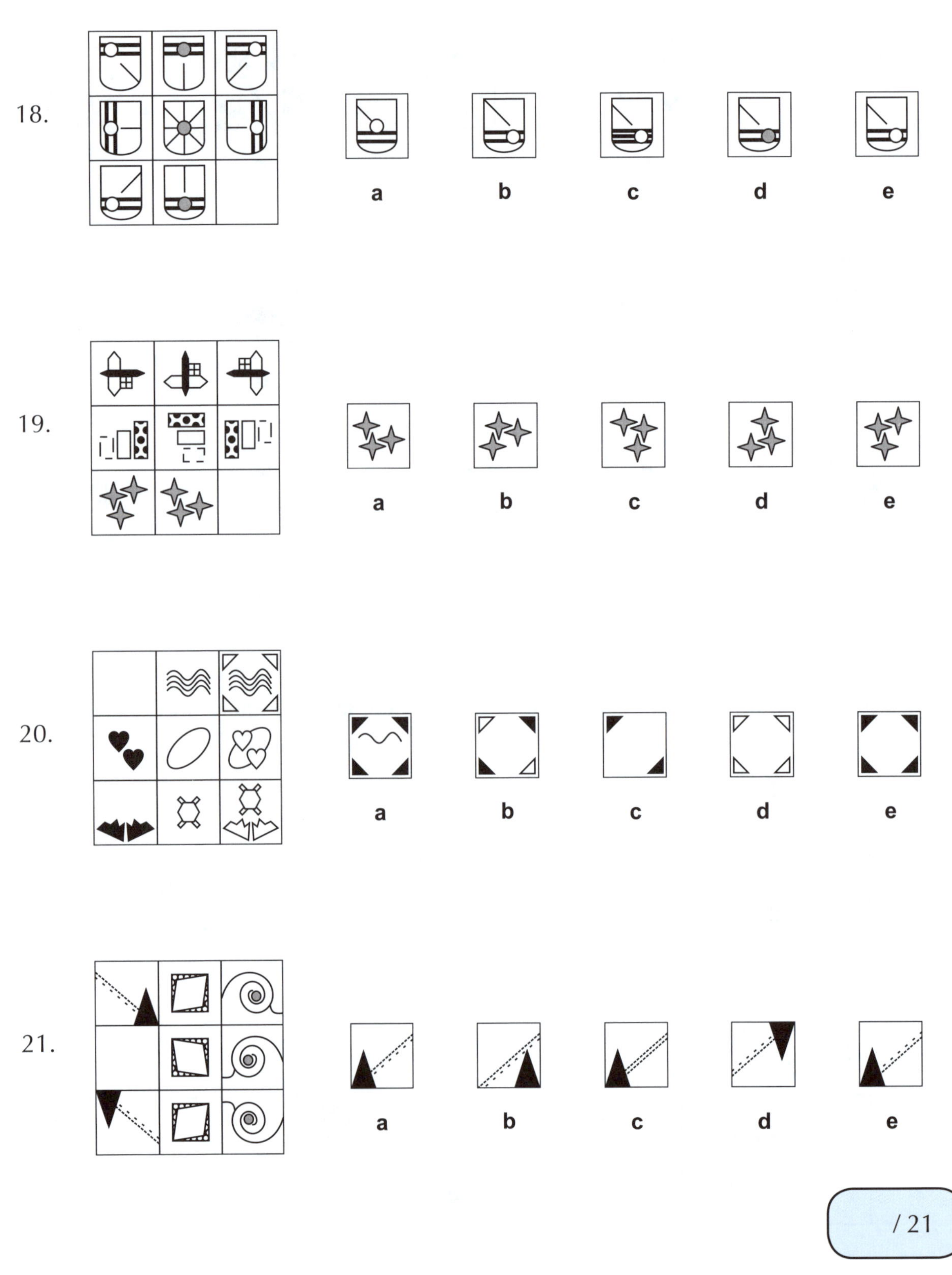

18.

19.

20.

21.

/ 21

These puzzles are a fun way to practise **spotting changes** and **word-making**.

Clothing Catastrophe

Colin has ruined two of his favourite T-shirts in the wash. Look at how the first T-shirt has changed, then match the second T-shirt to its ruined design.

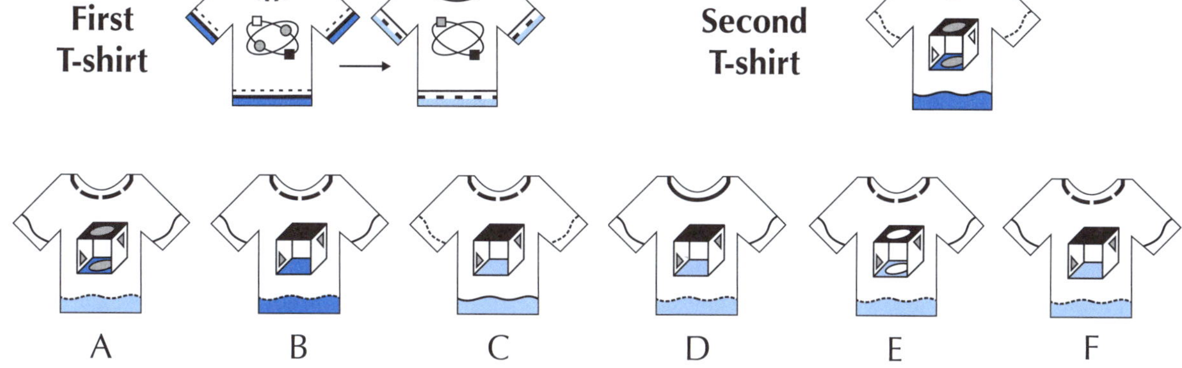

Word Storm

Help Marvin to find a path of words about **weather** in the group of letters on the right. You can move one step at a time in any direction. Each step can only be used once. Draw a line showing the correct path and fill in the words on the lines below.

S T O _ _ _

_ _ _ _ _ _

_ _ _ _ _ _ _

_ _ _ _ _ _ _ _

_ _ _ _ _ _ _

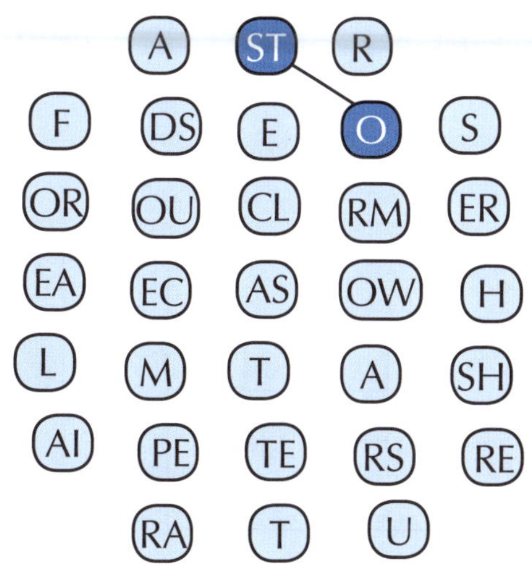

Workout 11

Q1-7 will test your **non-verbal reasoning** skills.
You have **4 minutes** to complete Q1-7.

Work out which option is a top-down 2D view of the 3D figure on the left.

1.  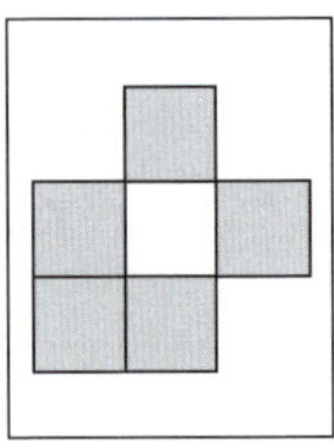  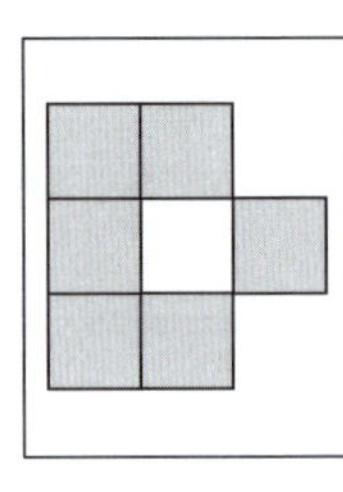 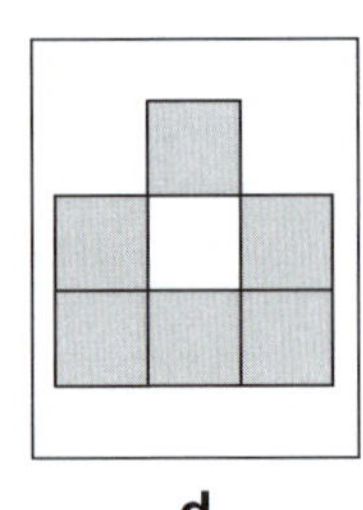

   a   b   c   d

2. 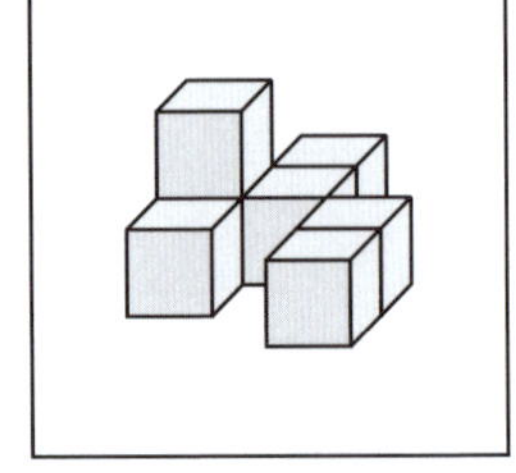 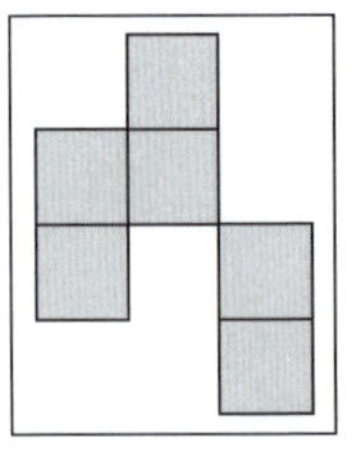 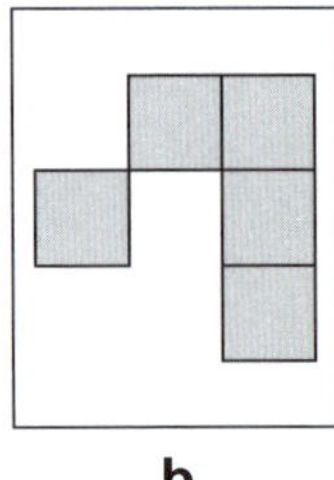 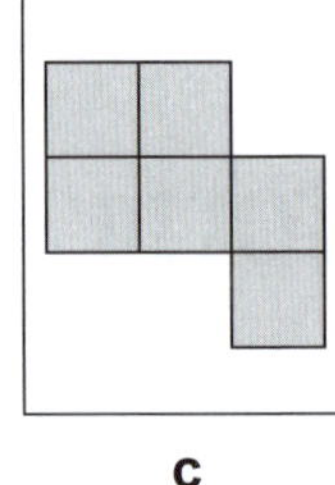 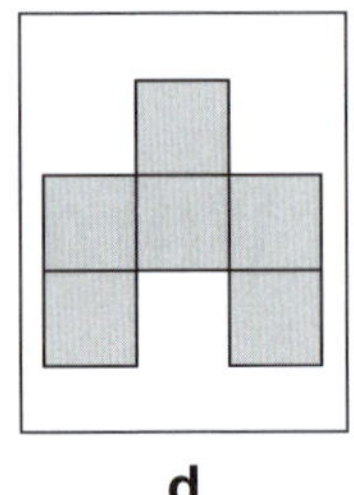

   a   b   c   d

3.  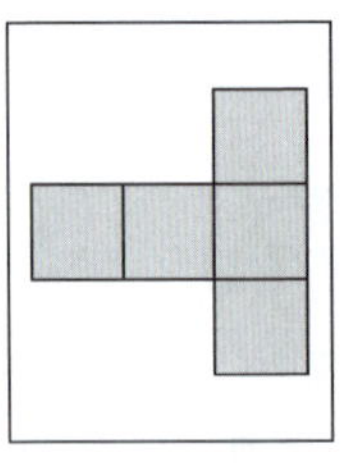  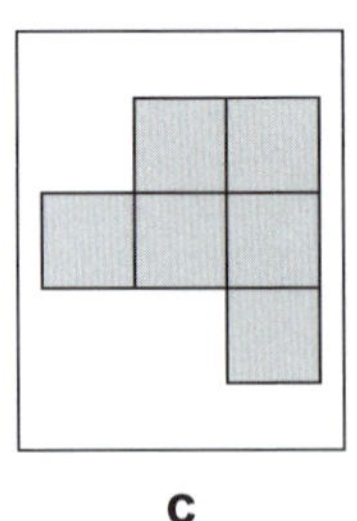 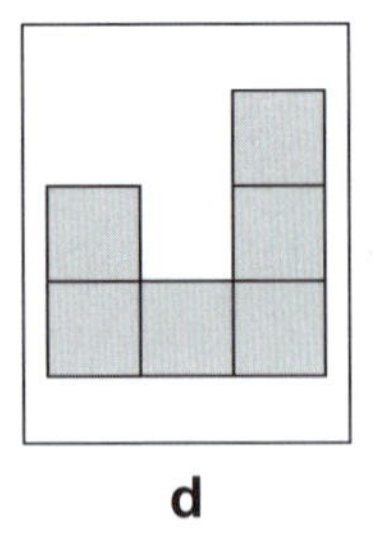

   a   b   c   d

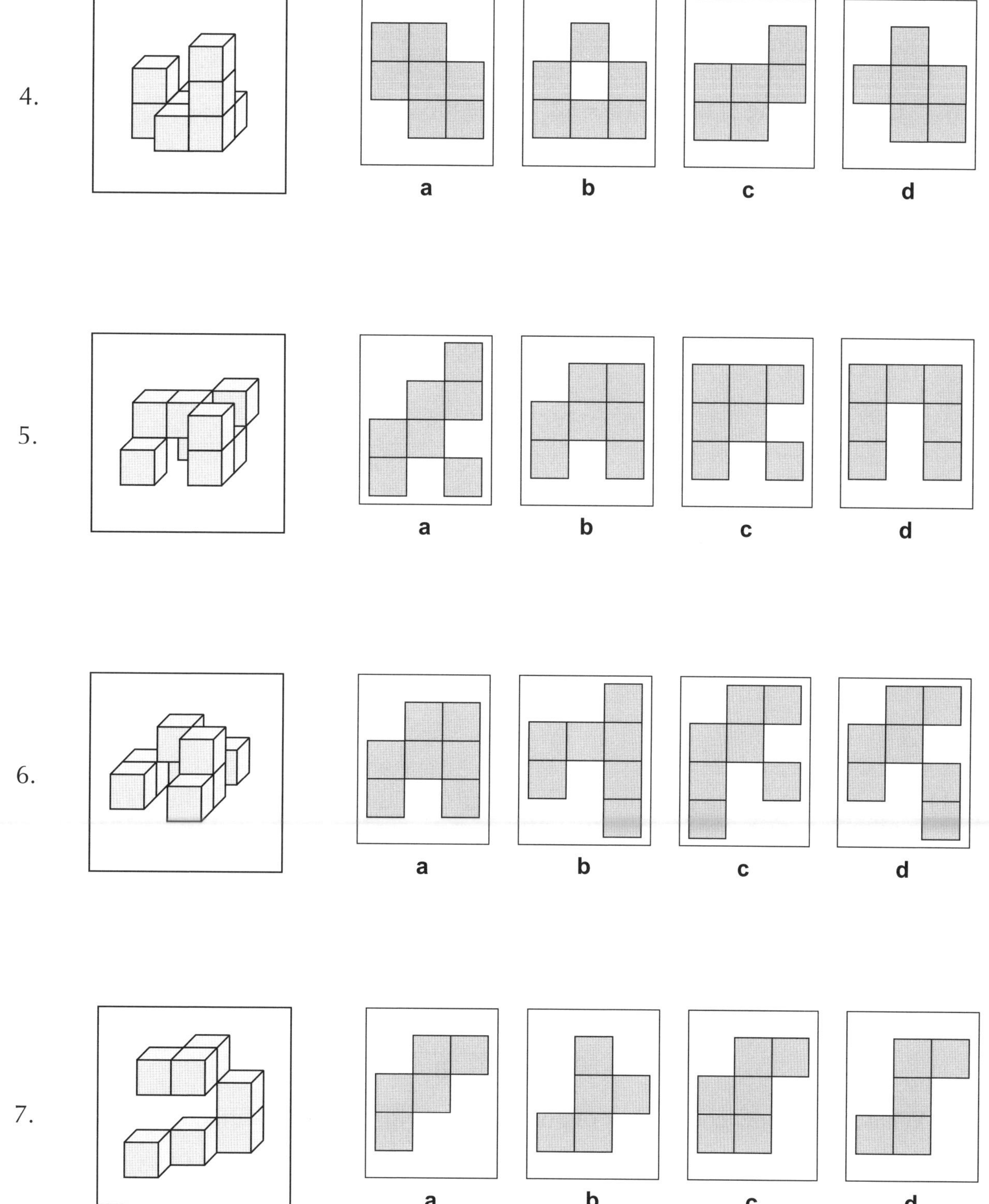

Workout 11

Q8-15 will test your **maths** skills.
You have **6 minutes** to complete Q8-15.

8. Use estimating to find 1218 × 52. Circle the correct option.

   A 1260   **C** 168 398   **E** 24 556
   B 43 116   **D** 63 336

9. The ratio of knives to forks in Sylvia's kitchen drawer is 3:2. There are 21 knives in the drawer. How many forks are in the drawer?

10. Norah is saving up to buy a table. So far she has saved £33.50, which is $\frac{1}{6}$ of the price of the table. What is the price of the table?

11. On the coordinate grid, the line is moved 2 units to the right and 3 units down.

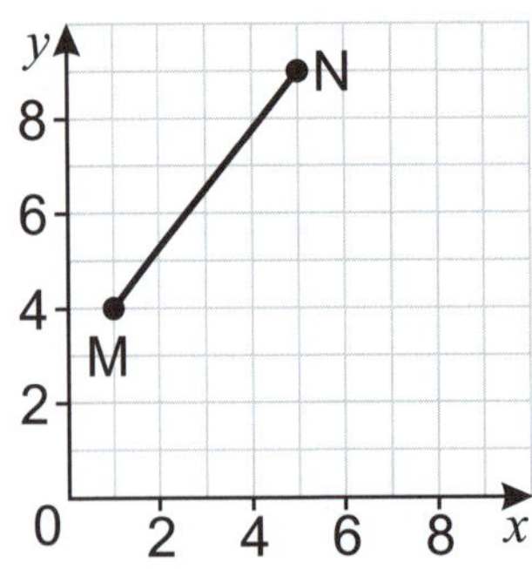

   What are the new coordinates of points M and N? Circle the correct option.

   A M(2, 8), N(6, 9)   **C** M(6, 8), N(7, 6)   **E** M(1, 3), N(6, 7)
   B M(3, 1), N(7, 6)   **D** M(3, 1), N(5, 7)

12. What is $215.8 \times 3.6 + 6.4 \times 215.8$?

13. Harvey earns money by mowing lawns. He charges 50 pence per m² of lawn that he mows. How much will he earn for mowing the lawn shown below?

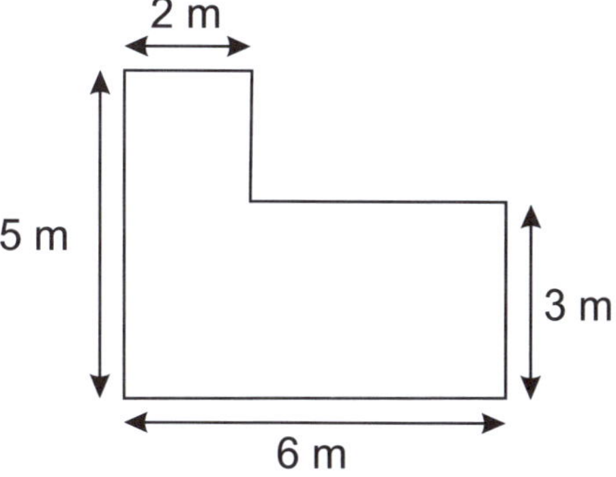

14. Dustin's book has 70 pages. He has read 65% of the pages. How many pages has he read?

15. The first four terms of a sequence are shown below.

$$3 + 2a, \quad 6 + 4a, \quad 9 + 6a, \quad 12 + 8a$$

If $a = 2$, what is the sixth number in the sequence?
Circle the correct option.

A 26	**C** 36	**E** 42
B 35	**D** 40	

/ 15

Workout 11

Q1-17 will test your **verbal reasoning** skills.
You have **6 minutes** to complete Q1-17.

In each question below, the words can be rearranged to form a sentence.
One word doesn't fit in the sentence. Underline the word that doesn't fit.

Example: red   the   has   <u>ride</u>   girl   bicycle   a

1. travel   flying   world   over   all   want   the   really   to   I

2. happy   with   my   me   smiles   playing   school   friends   makes

3. made   I   cupcakes   save   party   ate   the   nobody   those   that   for

4. invisible   make   to   camouflage   vanished   soldiers   the   helped   their

5. excel   ballerina   her   could   not   the   perform   routine   dance

Three of the words in each list are linked. Mark the word that is not related to these three.

Example: journal   diary   <u>textbook</u>   notebook

6. knoll   bank   mound   ravine

7. wire   cable   knot   lead

8. scatter   pepper   sprinkle   dip

9. secure   anchor   snatch   bind

10. crime   witness   officer   suspect

11. welder   plumber   electrician   apprentice

Complete the word on the right so that it means the opposite, or nearly the opposite, of the word on the left.

Example: heavy   l i g h t

12. ameliorate   ☐ o r s ☐ ☐

13. love   ☐ b ☐ ☐ r

14. sluggish   ☐ n e ☐ g ☐ t ☐ c

15. scarcity   a ☐ u n ☐ a ☐ ☐ e

16. delicate   d ☐ r ☐ b ☐ e

17. sceptic   b ☐ l ☐ ☐ ☐ e r

Q18-24 will test your **non-verbal reasoning** skills. You have **4 minutes** to complete Q18-24.

Work out which option would look like the figure on the left if it was reflected over the line.

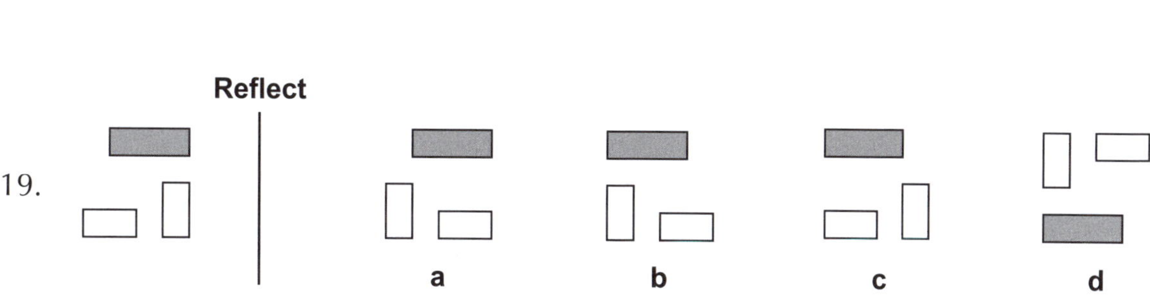

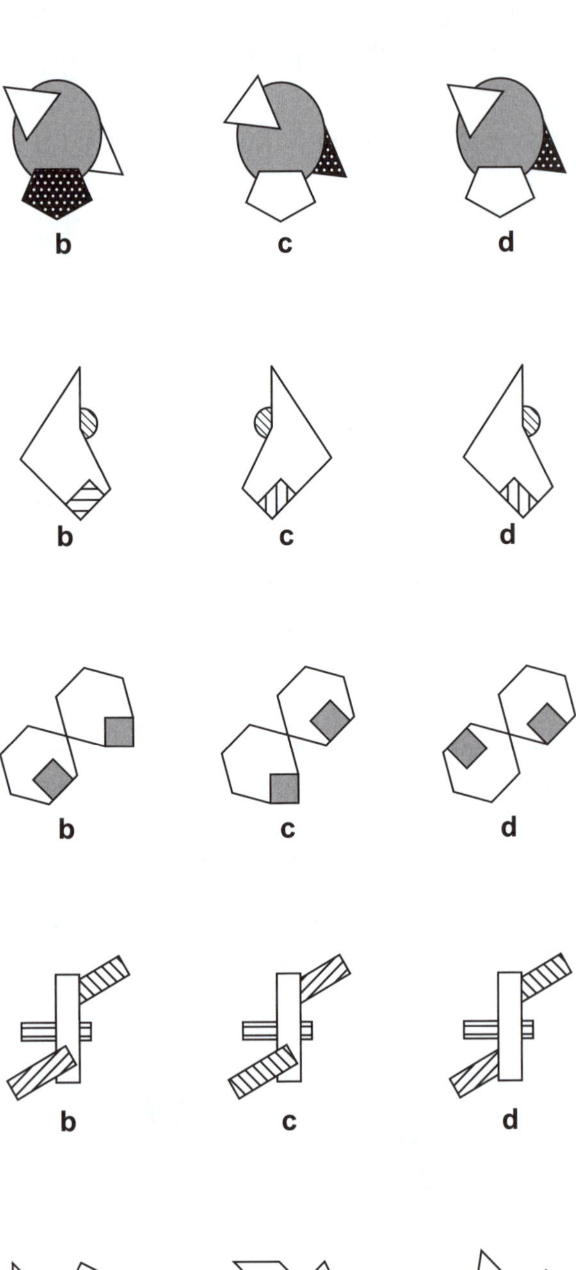

20. **Reflect**

| a | b | c | d |

21. **Reflect**

| a | b | c | d |

22. **Reflect**

| a | b | c | d |

23. **Reflect**

| a | b | c | d |

24. **Reflect**

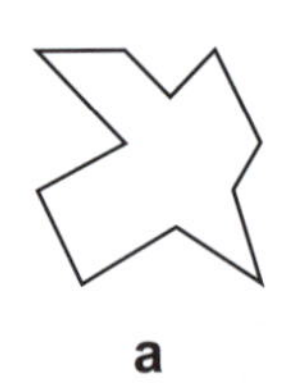 a b c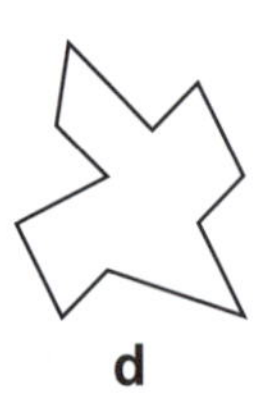 d

48

/ 24

10

Q1-7 will test your **maths** skills.
You have **6 minutes** to complete Q1-7.

1. Which of the following is not equivalent to 12? Circle the correct option.

   A 6 + 6   **C** 23 − 11   **E** −4 + 16

   B 5 + 7   **D** 33 − 22

2. Sebastian has £23.73 in his wallet. On his way to lunch he finds £5 on the floor and keeps it. He spends £7.28 on his lunch. How much money is left in Sebastian's wallet?

Jade is out running. The distance she has run is shown in the graph below.

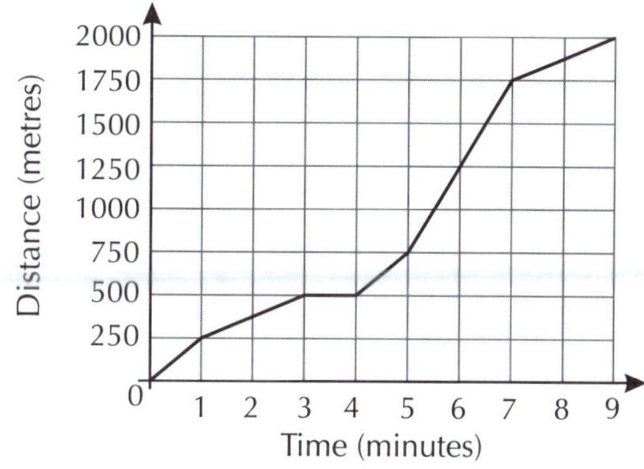

3. How far has Jade run in the last 4 minutes?

4. If Jade continues to run 2000 m every 9 minutes, how long would it take her to run 10 km?

49

5. The table shows the amount of water five people drank in a day.
    Use the approximation 1 pint ≈ 0.6 litres.

Ricardo	Ernest	Kat	Justin	Marshall
2.5 pints	3.7 pints	1.8 litres	2.4 litres	1 pint

Who drank the most water? Circle the correct option.

A Ricardo	**C** Kat	**E** Marshall
B Ernest	**D** Justin	

6. What is $\frac{1}{2} \div \frac{1}{8}$?

7. The diagram below shows a right-angled isosceles triangle.

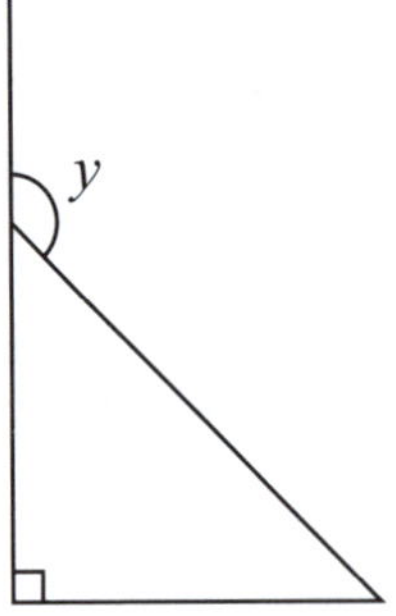

not drawn accurately

What is the size of angle y?

Mark the word outside the brackets that has a similar meaning to the words in both sets of brackets.

Example: (twig   branch)   (fasten   attach)   glue   <u>stick</u>   affix   bough

8.   (video   tape)   (chart   document)   shoot   archive   record   retain

9.   (circle   disc)   (stage   heat)   oval   spiral   phase   round

10.   (weave   wind)   (fibre   strand)   spin   thread   wire   braid

11.   (serious   important)   (unsmiling   sombre)   grave   muted   fatal   adverse

12.   (fee   tariff)   (count   tally)   index   account   tax   toll

13.   (waver   dither)   (stammer   stumble)   quiver   cower   falter   recoil

Find the word that means the same, or nearly the same, as the word on the left.

Example: **wide**   flat   straight   <u>broad</u>   long

14. **deafening**   boisterous   shrill   tumultuous   reverberating

15. **resolve**   extract   scheme   interpret   determine

16. **lustrous**   radiant   alluring   graceful   exquisite

17. **demolish**   depose   raze   deplete   collapse

18. **wicked**   morbid   grim   unbearable   heinous

19. **turmoil**   skirmish   setback   unrest   struggle

/ 19

Have a go at these puzzles for some fun with **spotting connections** and **3D shapes**.

A Sneaky Spider

Dress code

Webby Eight-Legs is trying to sneak into a celebrity spider party. There's a strict dress code, so Webby needs to make sure that she wears the correct outfit.

Which of Webby's outfits is most like the dress code?

A  B  C 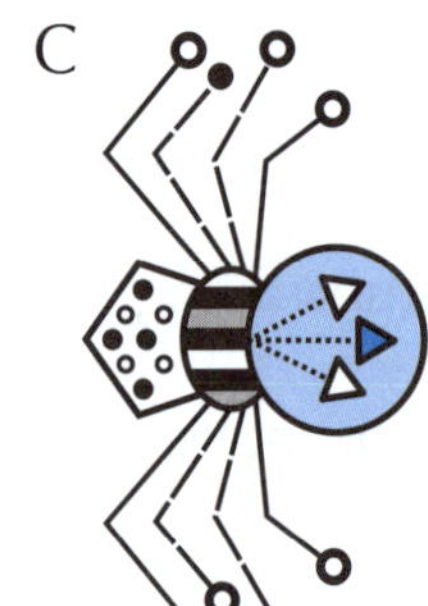 D 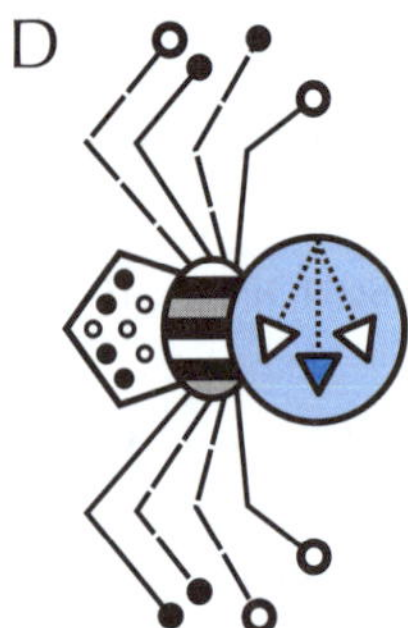

Cube Conundrum

Andrew builds a cube using identical smaller cubes. The cube he makes is 4 small cubes tall. Andrew then decides to paint a cross on each face of the new cube, as shown below. How many of the smaller cubes have 3 whole faces painted? How many cubes have an area equivalent to one face painted? How many cubes have no paint on them at all?

Q1-11 will test your **non-verbal reasoning** skills.
You have **6 minutes** to complete Q1-11.

Work out which of the four cubes can be made from the net.

1. 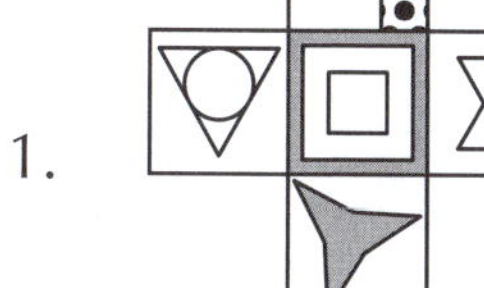    **a**    **b**    **c**   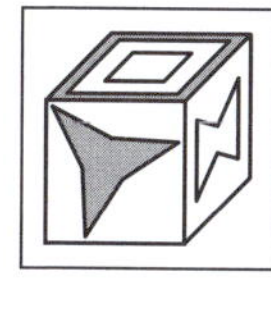 **d**

2. 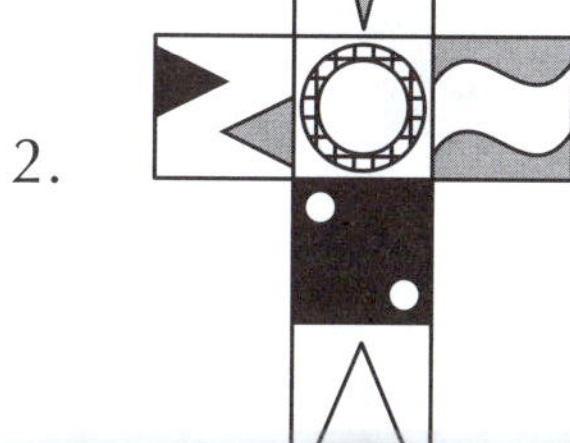    **a**   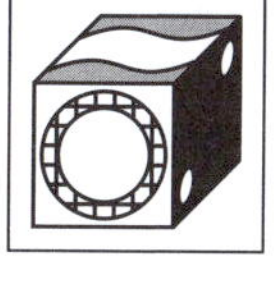 **b**    **c**    **d**

3. 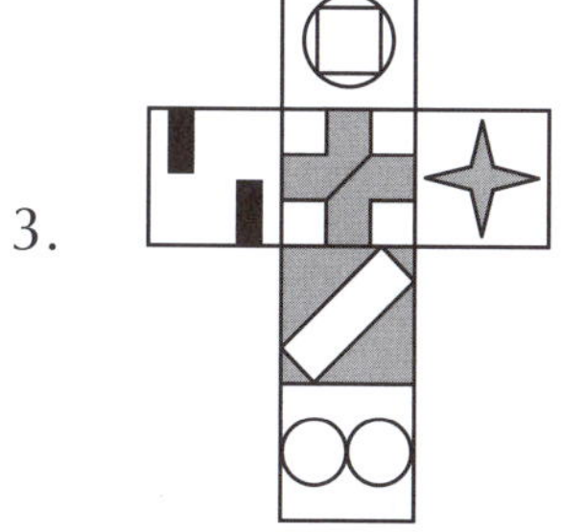   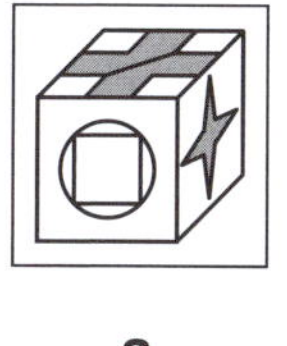 **a**    **b**    **c**    **d**

53

4. 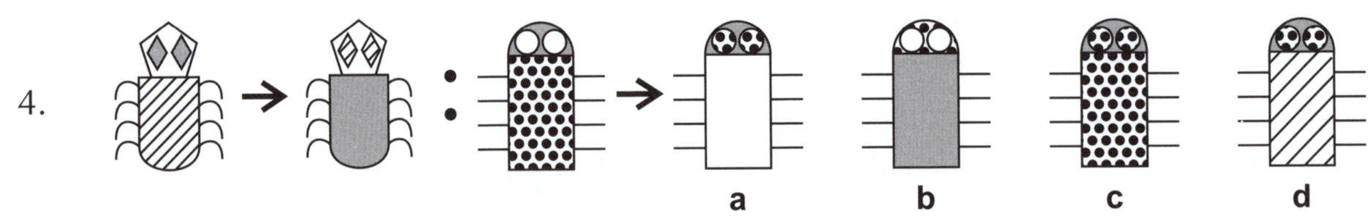

5. 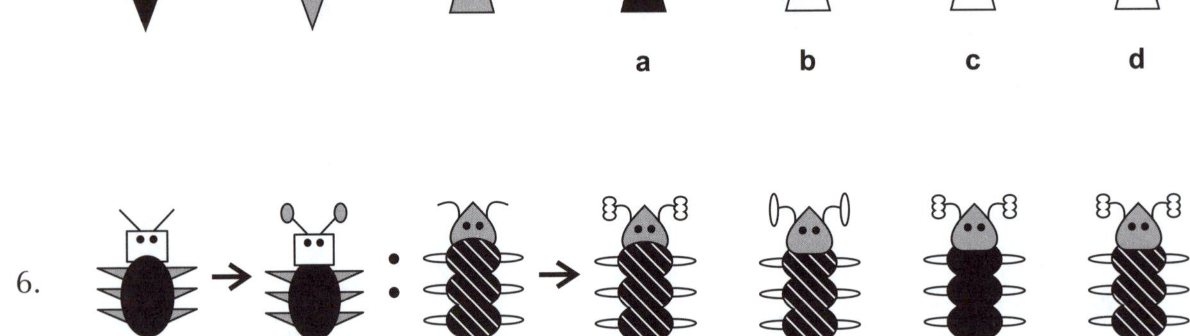

6.

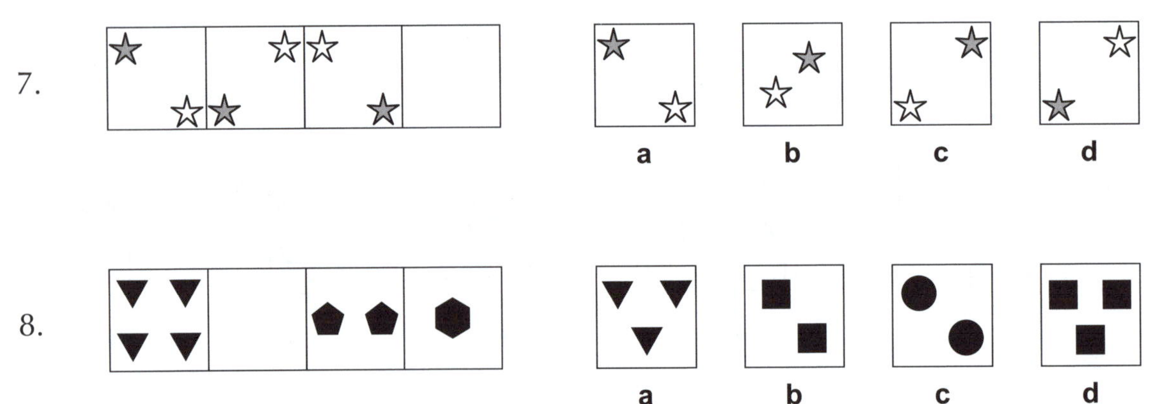

Work out which of the options best fits in place of the missing square in the series.

7.

8.

9. 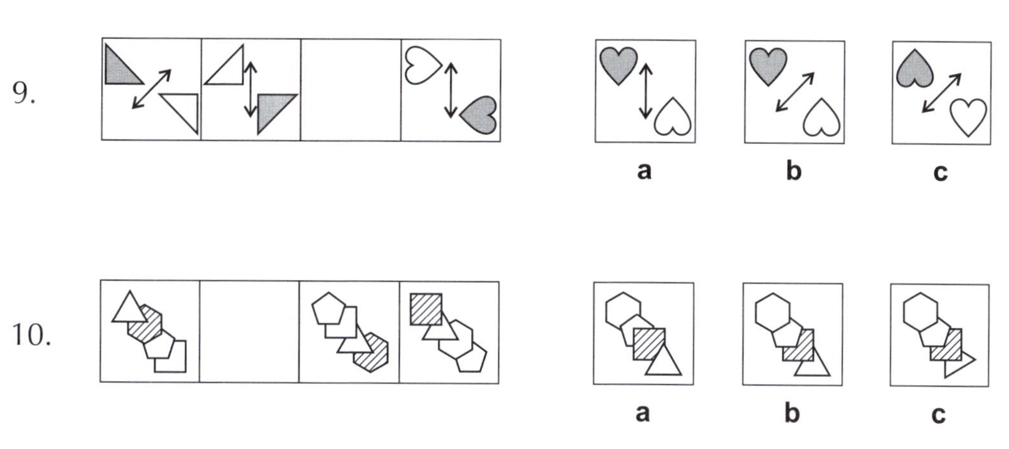

10.

11.

12. In which of the following does 7 have the lowest value? Circle the correct option.

    A   43 781

    B   239 973

    C   9789

    D   57 000

    E   971 063

13. Tessa runs 21 miles in 3 hours. On average how many miles did she run per hour?

miles

14. If the pentagon below was cut along all its lines of symmetry,
     how many pieces would there be?

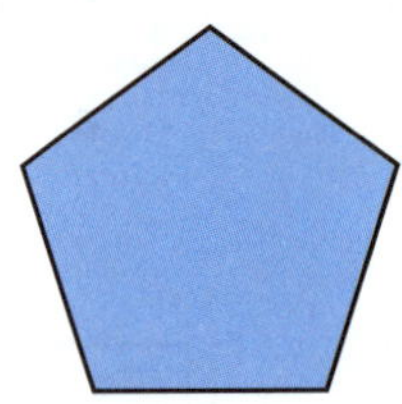

15. There are 300 steps leading to a temple. Each step is the same height and the
     height of 8 steps is 200 cm. Work out the total height of the steps.

m

16. Pierre and Carlo both go running. Pierre ran 20 km. Carlo ran 60% further
     than Pierre. How far did Carlo run?
     Use the approximation 8 km ≈ 5 miles. Circle the correct option.

A 7.5 miles	**C** 20 miles	**E** 32 miles
B 12.5 miles	**D** 30 km	

/ 16

> Q1-7 will test your **comprehension** skills.
> You have **6 minutes** to complete Q1-7.

Read this passage carefully and answer the questions that follow.

An abridged extract from 'In November'

With loitering step and quiet eye,
Beneath the low November sky,
I wandered in the woods, and found
A clearing, where the broken ground
5 Was scattered with black stumps and briers,
And the old wreck of forest fires.
It was a bleak and sandy spot,
And, all about, the vacant plot
Was peopled and inhabited
10 By scores* of mulleins** long since dead.
Not plants at all they seemed to me,
But rather some spare company
Of hermit folk, who long ago,
Wandering in bodies to and fro,
15 Had chanced upon this lonely way,
And rested thus, till death one day
Surprised them at their compline*** prayer,
And left them standing lifeless there.

There was no sound about the wood
20 Save the wind's secret stir. I stood
Among the mullein-stalks as still
As if myself had grown to be
One of their sombre company,
A body without wish or will
25 And as I stood, quite suddenly,
Down from a furrow in the sky
The sun shone out a little space
Across that silent sober place,
Over the sand heaps and brown sod,
30 The mulleins and dead goldenrod****,
And passed beyond the thickets grey,
And lit the fallen leaves that lay,
Level and deep within the wood,
A rustling yellow multitude.

Archibald Lampman

* scores — *a large number*

** mulleins — *flowering plants*

*** compline — *a Christian service that takes place in the evening*

**** goldenrod — *a plant with yellow flowers*

1. The narrator is walking "With loitering step" (line 1). What does this mean?

    A   The narrator often walks in the woods.

    B   The narrator intends to make trouble.

    C   The narrator is in pain.

    D   The narrator is walking slowly.

2. Which of the following statements best describes the clearing in lines 4-10?

    A   It is completely empty.

    B   It has been damaged by animals.

    C   It has been destroyed by fire.

    D   It used to be inhabited by people.

3. What does the word "bleak" (line 7) mean?

    A   Vivid   **C**   Disastrous

    B   Uneasy   **D**   Desolate

4. Which of the following statements about the narrator is true?

    A   He compares the plants in the clearing to people.

    B   He says a prayer in the clearing.

    C   He worries that someone is watching him.

    D   He meets some travellers in the woods.

5. Line 15 says "Had chanced upon this lonely way". What does this mean?

    A   Had hoped to cure loneliness

    B   Had accidentally found a secluded path

    C   Had felt very lucky

    D   Had enjoyed the solitude of the place

6. Which of the following is not mentioned in lines 19-34?

    A   The sound of the wind

    B   Dead plants

    C   A ray of sunlight

    D   Birds singing

7. What does "rustling yellow multitude" (line 34) refer to?

    A   The sun illuminating the woods

    B   Flowers in the undergrowth

    C   Leaves on the ground

    D   The sounds of woodland creatures

> Q8-14 will test your **non-verbal reasoning** skills.
> You have **4 minutes** to complete Q8-14.

Work out which option is most like the two figures on the left.

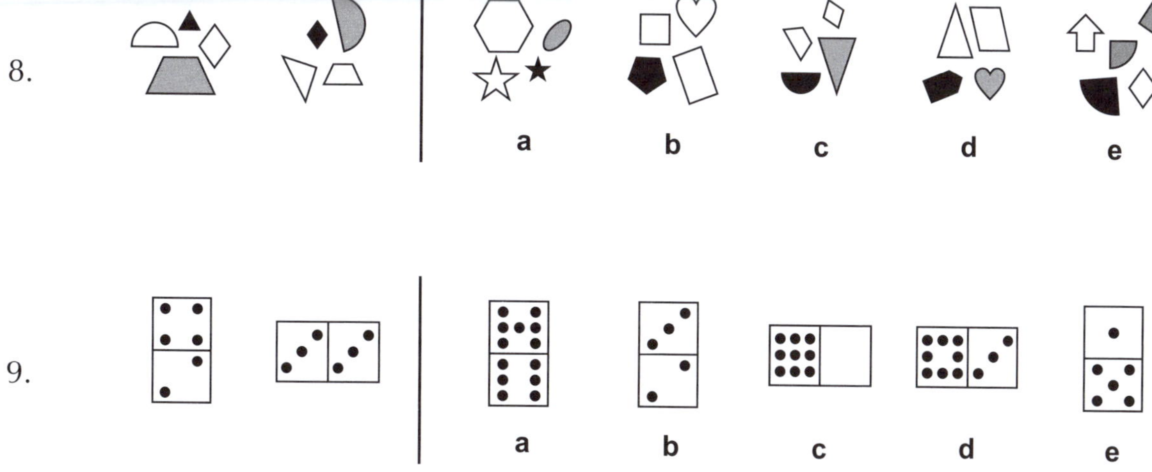

8.

        a   b   c   d   e

9.

        a   b   c   d   e

Workout 15

10. 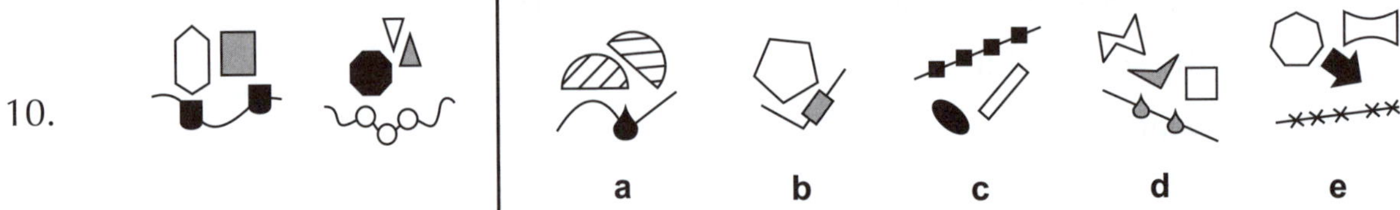

Work out which option would look like the figure on the left if it was rotated.

11.  Rotate

    a   b   c   d

12. 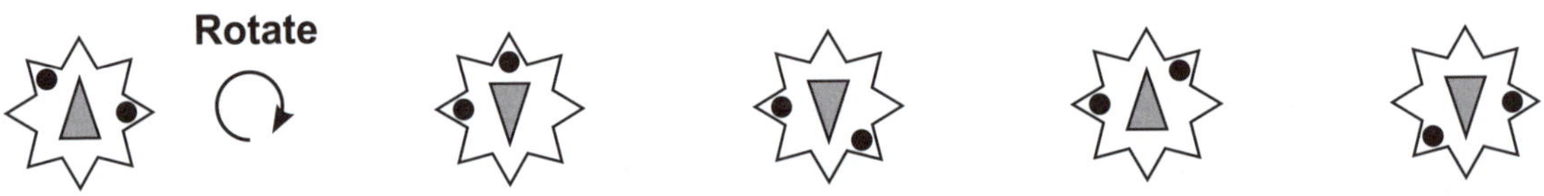 Rotate

    a   b   c   d

13.  Rotate

    a   b   c   d

14. 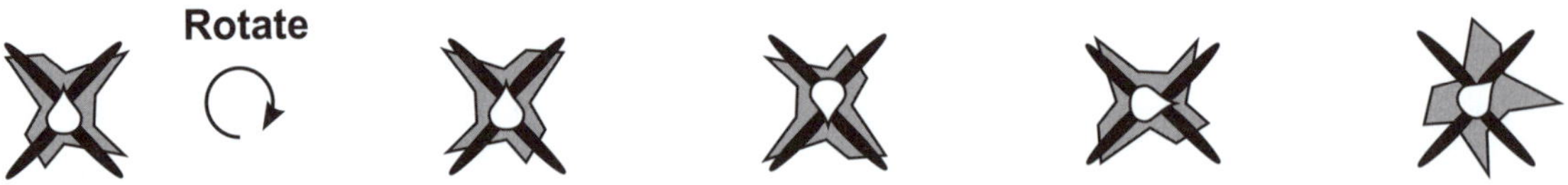 Rotate

    a   b   c   d

/ 14

10

Q1-5 will test your **maths** skills.
You have **4 minutes** to complete Q1-5.

1. What is $24 \div 6$? Give your answer in Roman numerals.

2. What is the volume of the cuboid shown below?

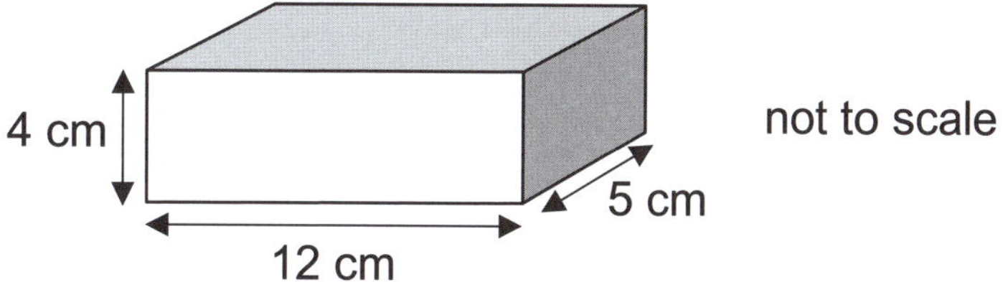

not to scale

 cm^3

3. Amelia had a summer job in August last year. She earned £41 a day and worked a total of 23 days. How much did she earn in total?

A	£892	**C**	£963	**E**	£1029
B	£943	**D**	£977		

4. If $x = 3$, which of the following numbers is equal to $x^2 + 3x$?
Circle the correct option.

A	6	**C**	12	**E**	18
B	9	**D**	15		

5. There are four difficulty levels of ski runs on a mountain and each level is represented by a colour. The pie chart shows the number of people that skied each colour of run in an hour, out of a total of 320. How many people skied on blue runs?

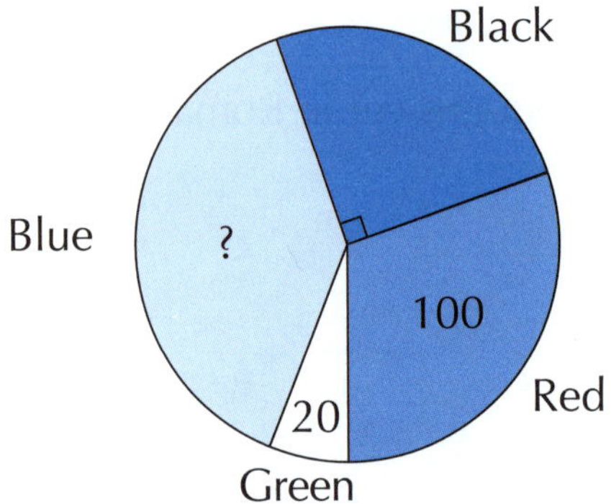

Q6-24 will test your **verbal reasoning** skills.
You have **6 minutes** to complete Q6-24.

Three of the words in each list are linked. Mark the word that is not related to these three.

Example: journal   diary   <u>textbook</u>   notebook

6. tundra   grassland   desert   territory

7. trot   canter   linger   gallop

8. zealous   empowered   passionate   avid

9. interval   epoch   age   era

10. adjacent   opposite   longer   above

Find the word that means the opposite, or nearly the opposite,
of the word on the left.

Example: **first**   later   <u>last</u>   next   beginning

11. **famished**   copious   ravenous   sated   mitigated

12. **idle**   influential   frivolous   driven   industrious

13. **civilised**   unkind   fierce   inhumane   barbaric

14. **untangle**   engage   entwine   extricate   encircle

15. **falsehood**   principle   fallacy   precision   verity

16. **honour**   fidelity   disgrace   renown   blemish

17. **disperse**   convene   enclose   mobilise   diffuse

Complete the word on the right so that it means the same,
or nearly the same, as the word on the left.

Example: scared   a f r a i d

18. hypnotise   m _ s _ _ r _ s e

19. outline   s _ l h _ u _ t _ e

20. dubious   d _ u _ _ _ u l

21. unimportant   n _ g _ i g _ b l e

22. negotiate   _ _ g _ l e

23. spirited   a _ i m _ _ e d

24. profusion   _ u _ t i _ u _ e

/ 24

Workout 16

Puzzles 6

These puzzles are a great way to practise your **word-making** and **algebra** skills.

Wobbly Words

Fill in the missing words in the rickety rope bridges. Each word is one letter different from the previous word. Some words have been filled in for you.

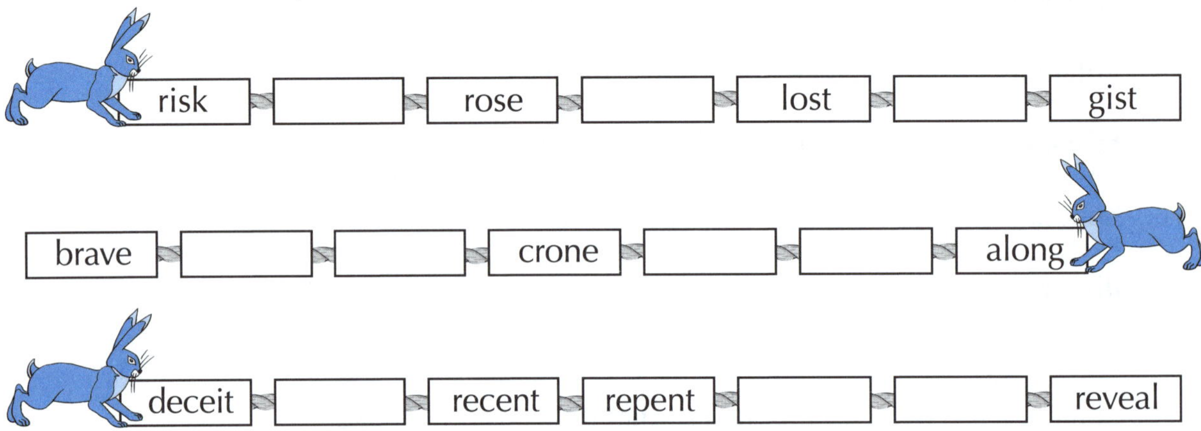

Combination Calculation

Esteban is always forgetting the combination to his safe, so he wrote some clues to help himself remember:

- The first number is the smallest prime number multiplied by the second smallest prime number.

- The second number is the number of degrees in a right angle divided by 30.

- If the second number is x then the third number is $\frac{x}{5} + \frac{14}{10}$.

- If the third number is y then the fourth number is $4y - (3 + y)$.

What is Esteban's combination?

Q1-10 will test your **verbal reasoning** skills.
You have **4 minutes** to complete Q1-10.

Fill in the missing letters to complete the words in the following passage.

Since the Ancient Greek philosopher Plato wrote about the city of Atlantis over

1. 2000 years ago, it has c a ☐ t i ☐ ☐ t e d people around the world.

2. Atlantis was said to have been a mighty and ☐ r ☐ s p ☐ ☐ o u s

3. civilisation, but its r ☐ s ☐ d ☐ ☐ t s were believed to have greatly

4. angered their gods with increasingly i ☐ m ☐ ☐ a l behaviour. As a

5. punishment, the gods ☐ u ☐ m e ☐ ☐ e d Atlantis beneath the sea.

Many people have searched for the lost city and its treasures, but with no

6. success. Very ☐ i ☐ t ☐ e trustworthy evidence about the location

7. of Atlantis exists, although several ☐ n ☐ r ☐ v ☐ n theories have been

proposed by historians and Atlantis enthusiasts alike. It is now thought that if

8. Atlantis did exist, a volcanic e ☐ u ☐ ☐ i o ☐ is more likely to have

9. been responsible for its c a ☐ a s t ☐ o ☐ ☐ i c end than any

kind of divine intervention. Although most agree that Atlantis was nothing more

10. than a myth, ☐ p ☐ c ☐ l a ☐ i o n remains rife about exactly

where this legendary city might lie hidden beneath the waves.

Players in a quiz gain 2 points for answering a question correctly and lose 1 point for answering one incorrectly. The scores of five players halfway through the quiz are shown below.

Derek	Iris	Orla	Anderson	Martha
0	2	−3	11	−6

11. If Orla gets four questions wrong in a row, what will her score be?
Circle the correct option.

A   1   **C**   −1   **E**   −11

B   −4   **D**   −7

12. In the second half, Iris doesn't play and Martha gets every question correct.
After how many questions did Martha catch up with Iris's score?

13. The diagram below shows a net for a square-based pyramid, where the triangular faces are equilateral. What is the perimeter of the net?

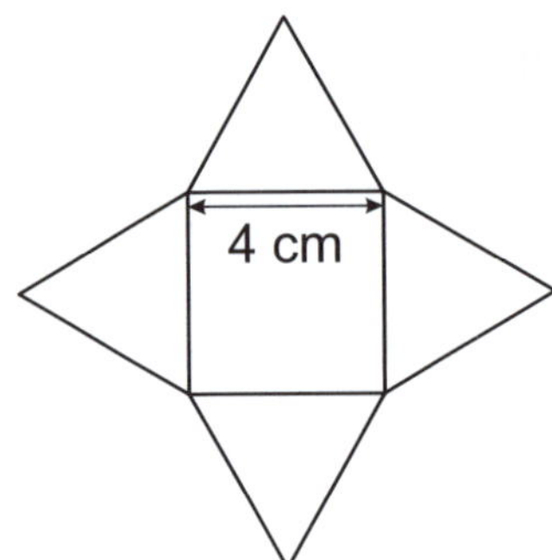

cm

14. $5698 \div 56 = 101.75$. What is $5698 \div 5600$?

15. A ferry journey is 6 hours and 40 minutes long. Theo has been on the ferry
for 5 hours. What percentage of the journey has he already completed?
Circle the correct option.

A 90%	**C** 85%	**E** 75%
B 70%	**D** 60%	

16. The prices of two holidays are shown in the table below.

Holiday	Flights	Per Day
Spain	£230	£50
Greece	£320	£30

What is the difference in the total price between the two holidays for
seven days? Circle the correct option.

A £90	**C** £10	**E** £70
B £50	**D** £30	

17. The diagram shows a rectangular picture frame. The shaded
border of the frame is made from 5 cm wide pieces of wood.
What is the area of the shaded border of the frame?

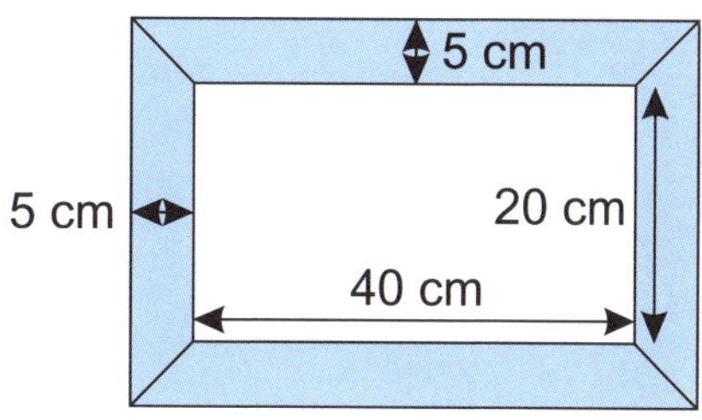

cm²

/ 17

Workout 18

Q1-11 will test your **non-verbal reasoning** skills.
You have **6 minutes** to complete Q1-11.

Work out which of the options best fits in place of the missing hexagon in the grid.

1. 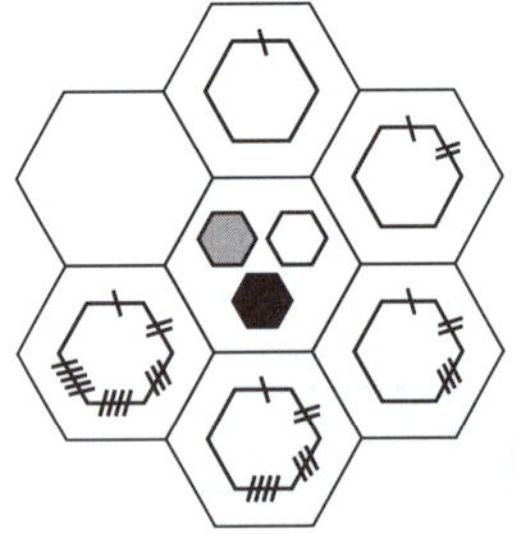  a 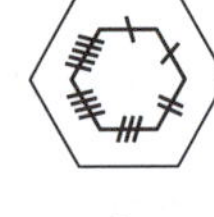 b  c 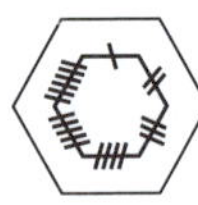 d

2. 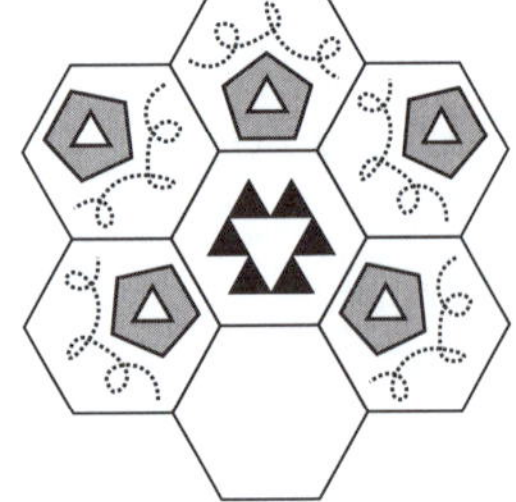  a 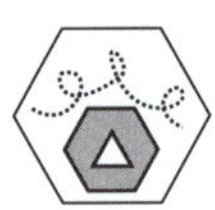 b 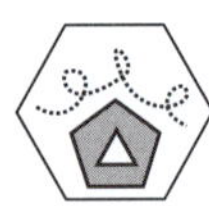 c  d

3. 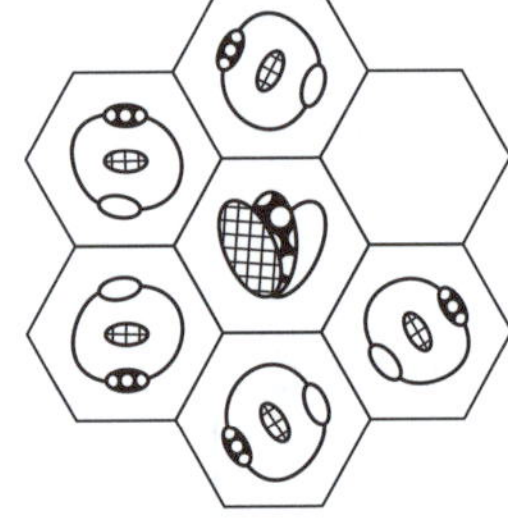 a  b  c 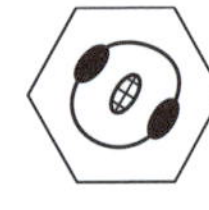 d

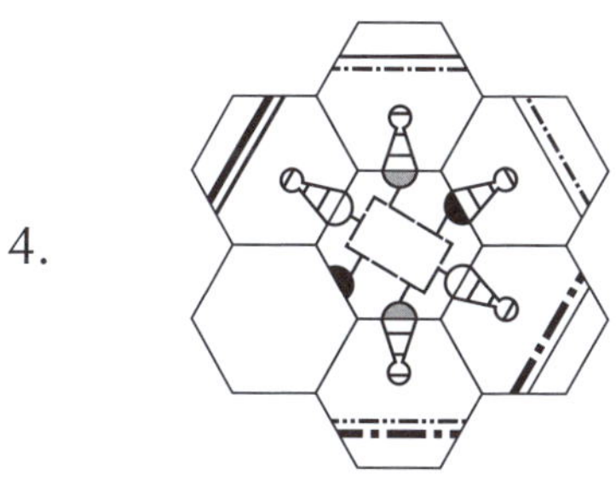 4.

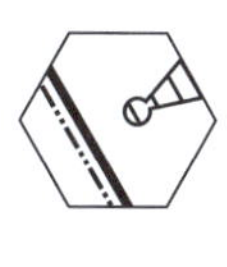 **a**    **b**   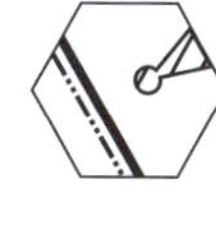 **c**    **d**

Work out which of the four cubes can be made from the net.

 5.

 **a**    **b**    **c**    **d**

6.

 **a**    **b**    **c**    **d**

7.

 **a**    **b**    **c**    **d**

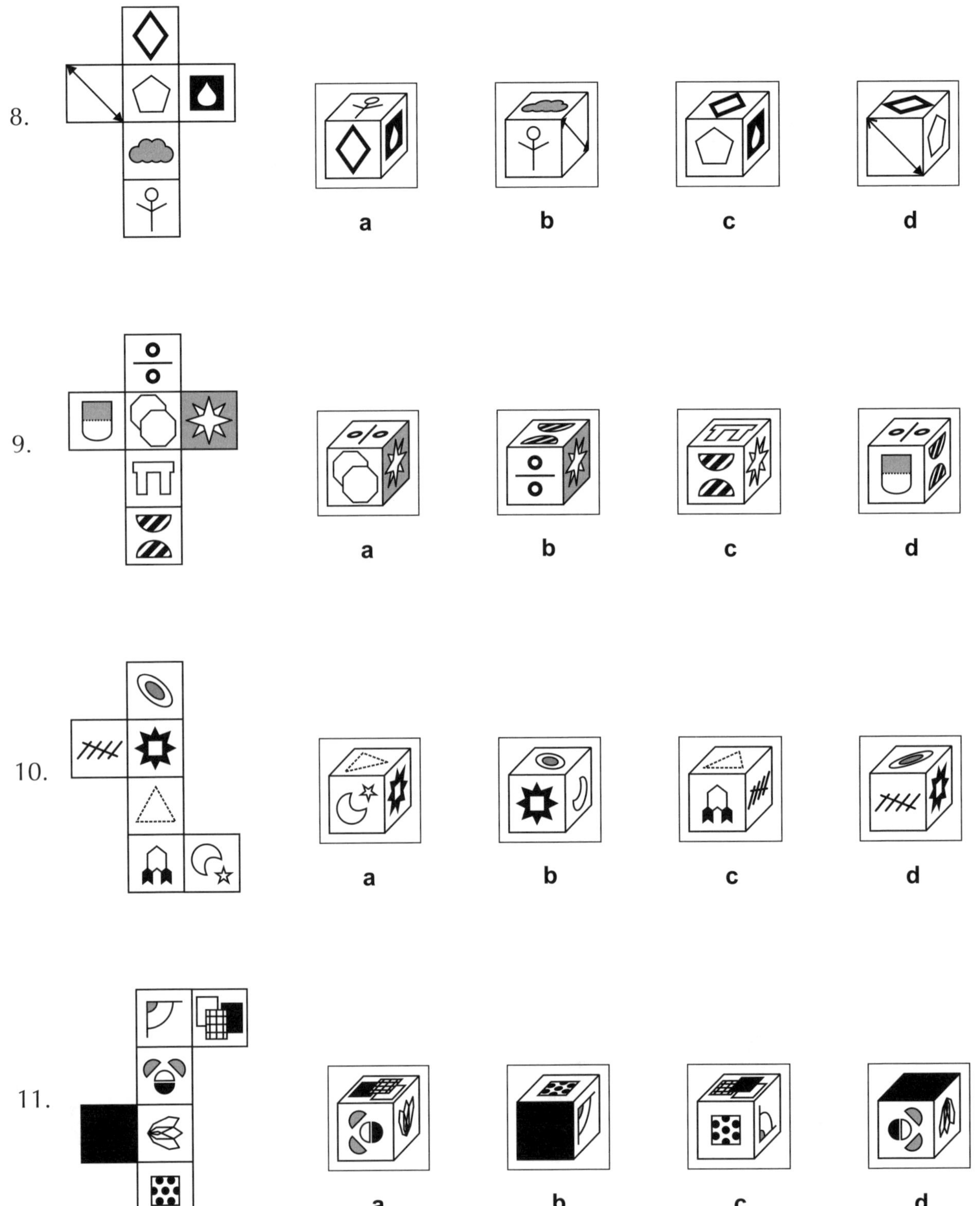

8.

9.

10.

11.

70

In each question below, the words can be rearranged to form a sentence.
One word doesn't fit in the sentence. Underline the word that doesn't fit.

Example: red   the   has   <u>ride</u>   girl   bicycle   a

12. planes   loved   the   people   teaching   pilot   fly   to   learnt   how

13. thousand   over   growth   live   can   trees   one   oak   for   years

14. lots   cheek   saved   hamsters   store   pouches   their   in   food   can   of

15. Queen   swans   English   crown   Her   to   belong   the   Majesty   many

16. way   anyone   this   was   could   there   prepared   must   have   for   no

17. burglar   a   police   testimony   crime   Mark's   the   helped   catch   to

Mark the word outside the brackets that has a similar meaning to the words in
both sets of brackets.

Example: (twig   branch)   (fasten   attach)   glue   <u>stick</u>   affix   bough

18. (tedious   tiresome)   (dreary   colourless)   stale   plain   passive   dull

19. (tremble   vibrate)   (unnerve   scare)   shake   bother   faze   distress

20. (swelling   pimple)   (churn   seethe)   steam   flare   ulcer   boil

21. (carry   convey)   (support   brace)   tote   endure   bear   reinforce

22. (valley   depression)   (vessel   bowl)   basin   gully   tank   ditch

23. (screen   mask)   (cape   robe)   cover   shawl   cloak   facade

/ 23

Workout 19

Q1-7 will test your **non-verbal reasoning** skills.
You have **4 minutes** to complete Q1-7.

Work out which set of blocks can be put together to make the 3D figure on the left.

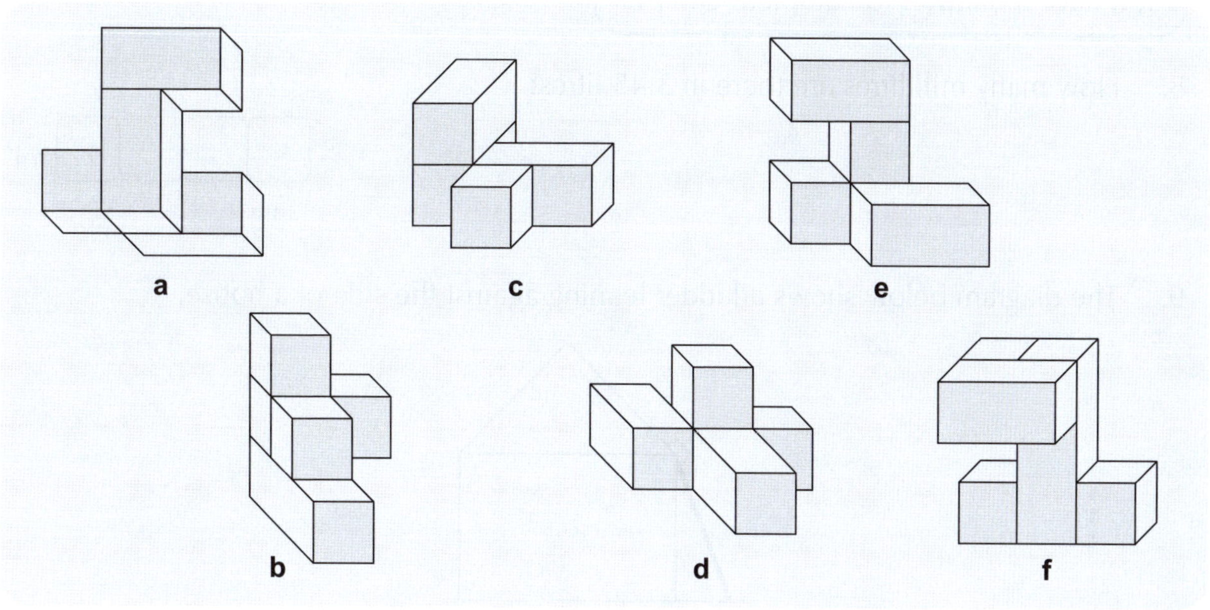

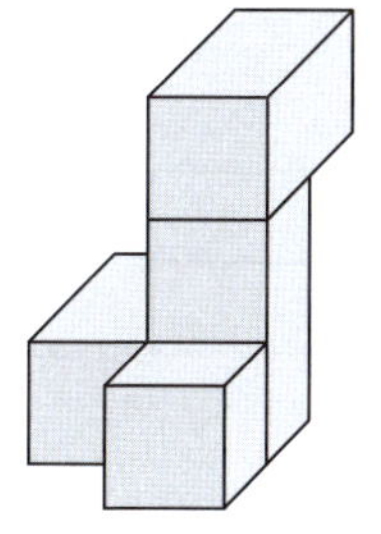

4.

a   d

b   e

c   f

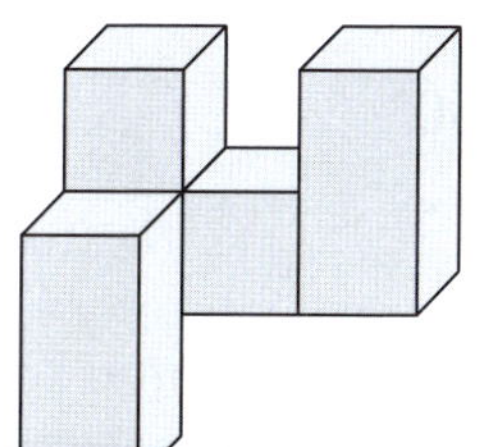

5.

a   d

b   e

c   f

6.

a   d

b   e

c   f

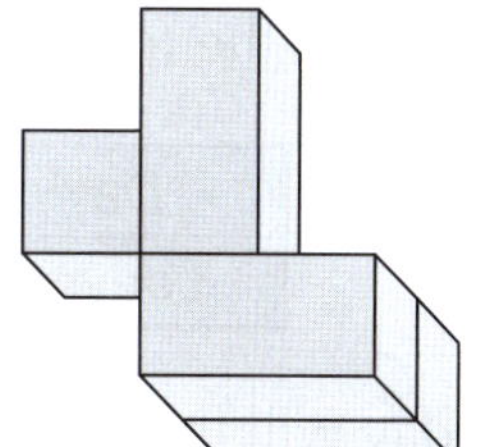

7.

a   d

b   e

c   f

8. How many millilitres are there in 3.45 litres?

ml

9. The diagram below shows a ladder leaning against the side of a house.

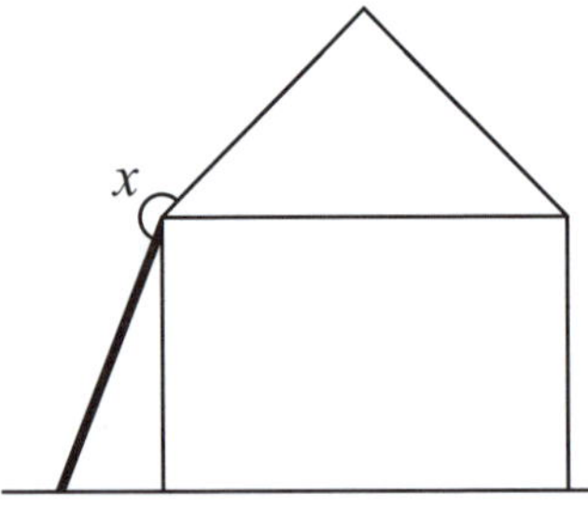

Which of the following is the most likely size of angle *x*? Circle the correct option.

A	203°	**C**	175°	**E**	86°
B	250°	**D**	157°		

10. What is 36% of 800?

11. A tree sheds exactly half its leaves every day. The table below shows the number of leaves left on the tree at the end of the first 3 days.

Day	1	2	3
Leaves	96	48	24

On what day will the tree have an odd number of leaves left?

Day

12. Jonathan is sorting out his recycling. He has 15 plastic items, 8 tins and
4 glass items. What proportion of Jonathan's recycling items are plastic?
Circle the correct option.

A	$^2/_5$	**C**	$^{13}/_{27}$	**E**	$^5/_9$
B	$^1/_2$	**D**	$^2/_3$		

13. Hassan lives 8 miles from school. If Hassan travels 12 miles per hour on his bike
how long will it take him to cycle to school? Circle the correct option.

A   20 minutes
B   45 minutes
C   30 minutes
D   15 minutes
E   40 minutes

14. The diagram below shows a fan. The fan has a diameter of $4a$ cm. The fan blades
are equilateral triangles.

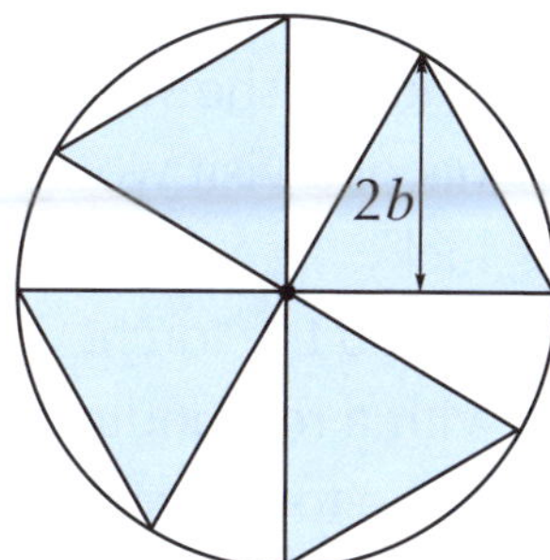

Which of the following expressions describes the area of the shaded fan blades?
Circle the correct option.

A	$16ab$	**C**	$8ab$	**E**	$6a^2$
B	$^1/_2a + 4b$	**D**	$4a + 2b$		

/ 14

Workout 19

Q1-7 will test your **comprehension** skills.
You have **6 minutes** to complete Q1-7.

Read this passage carefully and answer the questions that follow.

The Old Well

The hundred-year-old well was an incongruous piece of history on the edge of a
housing estate that had existed for less than a decade. Stones were missing from the
once-neat circle, and there was a thick coating of moss around its rim. When you
peered over the edge, you couldn't see the bottom — there was only a deep, fierce
5   darkness that seemed to go on forever.

    Alice's brother Chris — who always thought he knew best — claimed that it was
a portal to another world. He said aliens and monsters crawled out of it at night and
skulked back down at sunrise. Alice had made it her mission to find out for herself,
even though Chris had scoffed that the monsters were far too clever to be caught.

10   She shone her torch down into the well's unfathomable depths. The council had
installed a spindly grate over the top after local residents complained it was a hazard.
Monsters probably weren't fazed by the council's health and safety measures though.
Through the grate, Alice's torch illuminated the sludge and grime of the discoloured
stone walls, but not much else. She knew she would never get a sighting of a monster
15   in the daytime, but perhaps remnants of a visit would survive — a scale or a feather, or
maybe even a footprint if she was lucky.

    Alice's hand slipped and she dropped the torch. It lurched through the holes in the
grate and tumbled down the well with a resounding clatter, banging against the stone
walls. Alice's heart was pounding. She took a step back. A low, thunderous rumble
20   was rising from deep within the well.

1. Which of the following statements must be false?

    A   It is difficult to see inside the well.

    B   There is vegetation growing on the well.

    C   The housing estate was built before the well.

    D   The well is located near an urban area.

2. Which of the following words best describes the condition of the well?

    A   Intact   **C**   Imposing

    B   Dilapidated   **D**   Resplendent

3. How does Chris feel about Alice's attempt to investigate the well?

    A   He is supportive of her efforts.

    B   He is sceptical about her plan.

    C   He is worried for her safety.

    D   He wants to find the monsters first.

4. Why is there a grate on top of the well?

    A   To prevent monsters climbing out.

    B   To stop people investigating the well.

    C   To prevent accidents.

    D   To preserve the well.

5. According to the text, what does Alice hope to prove from her investigation?

    A   That a monster has been at the well.

    B   That she isn't afraid of monsters.

    C   That monsters can have feathers or scales.

    D   That the well is a dangerous place.

6. Which of the following must be true?

   A   The torch is caught by the metal grate.

   B   Alice reaches down into the well to get her torch.

   C   The torch illuminates the bottom of the well.

   D   The torch makes a lot of noise as it falls.

7. How do you think Alice feels in line 19?

   A   Curious

   B   Ecstatic

   C   Alarmed

   D   Nonchalant

> Q8-14 will test your **non-verbal reasoning** skills.
> You have **4 minutes** to complete Q8-14.

Work out which option is most like the three figures on the left.

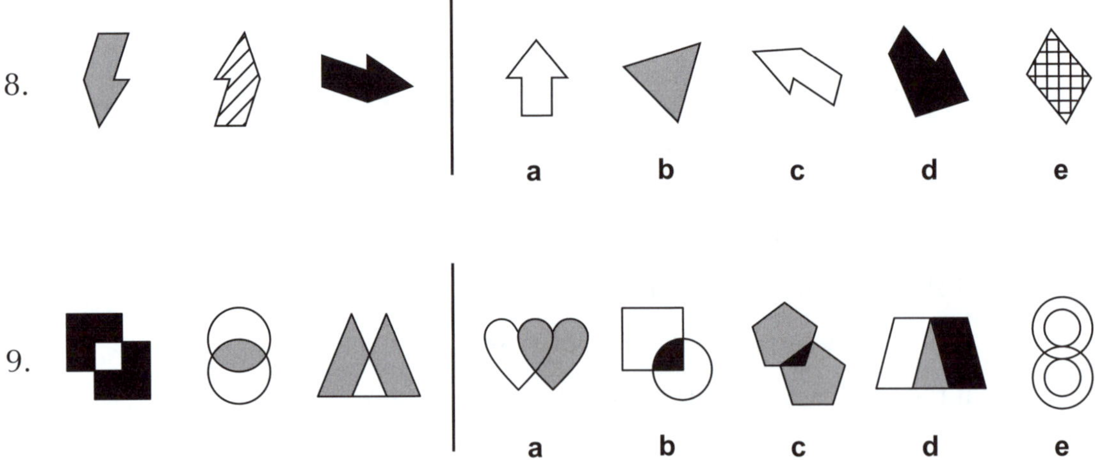

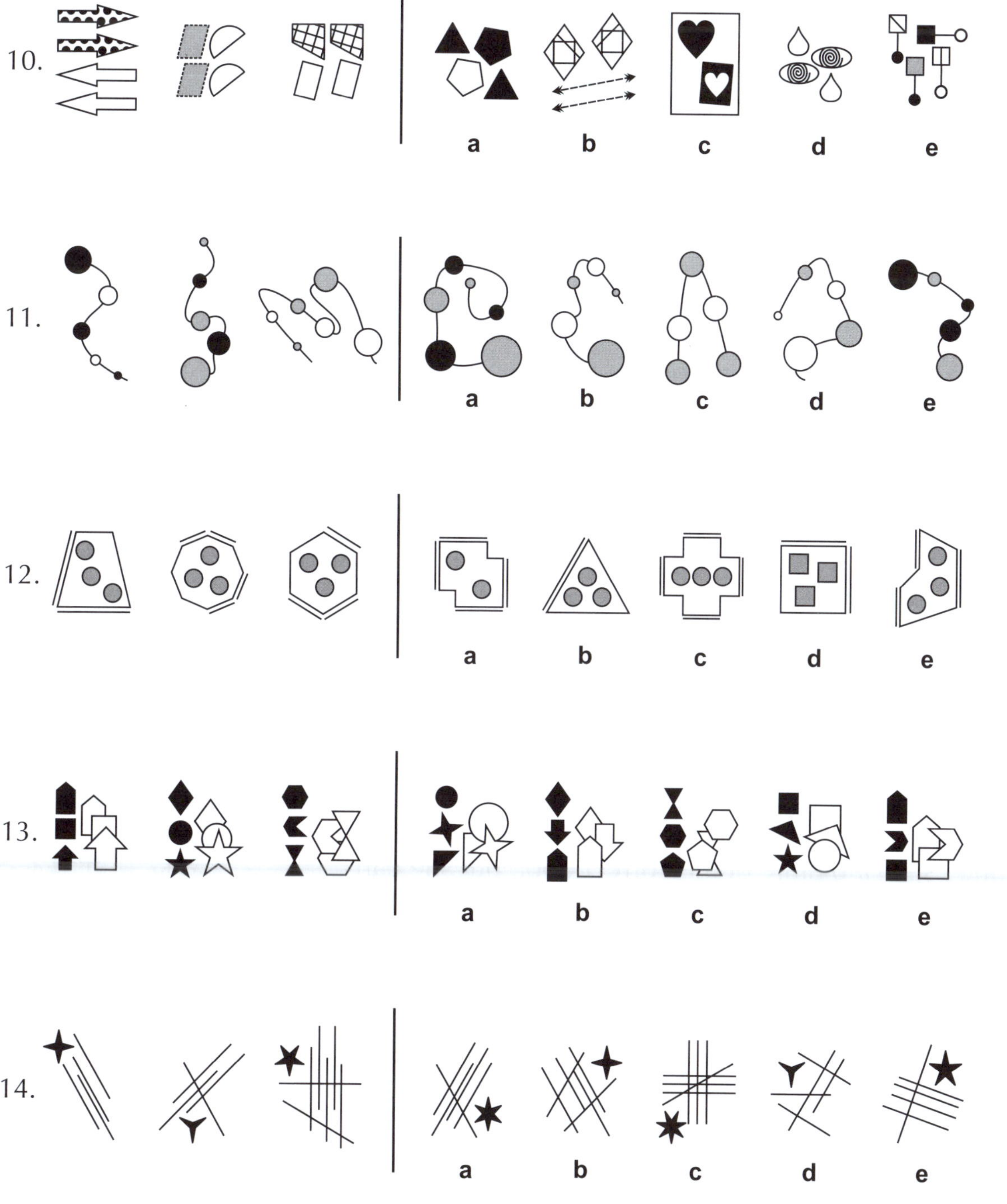

10.

11.

12.

13.

14.

Workout 20

/ 14

Try these puzzles for a fun way to practise your **vocabulary** and **symmetry** skills.

Typo Trouble

Basil is typing up a book, but he's made some mistakes.
Change one letter in each word on the books below so that it
matches the definition beneath it, and write the correct word on the line.

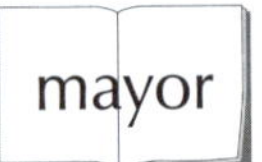

mayor

great or crucial

____

object

completely awful

____

torrent

severe suffering

____

health

a fireplace

____

accept

a way of speaking

____

grate

extremely angry

____

chapter

to speak quickly

____

nature

fully grown

____

Mirror, Mirror...

Lucy is trying to escape a magical mansion.
She's seen a picture of the correct door, but she can
only search for it using a mirror or she'll be turned to
stone. She's seen four doors through the mirror.
Which is the correct one?

The correct door

A
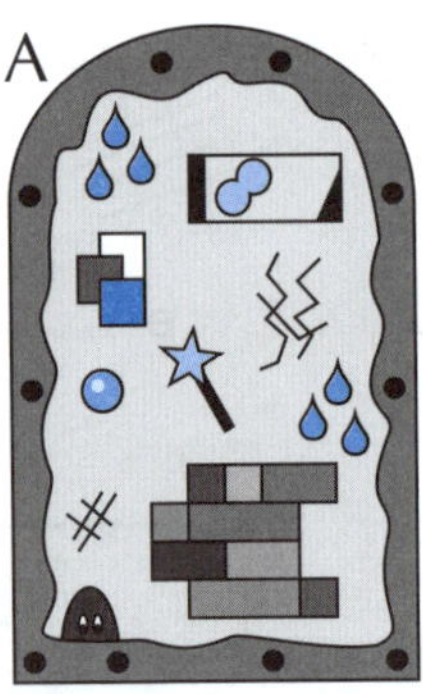

B

C

D

Q1-7 will test your **maths** skills.
You have **6 minutes** to complete Q1-7.

1. Round 179 502 to the nearest thousand.

2. Work out the angle labelled x.

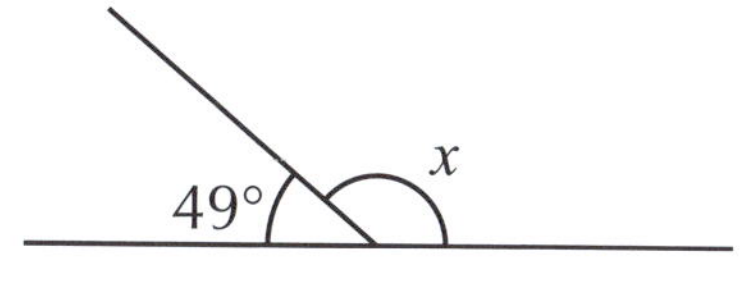

Aziz records the number of visits to his bird feeder by different types of birds. In total he records 72 visits to his bird feeder. His results are shown in the bar chart below.

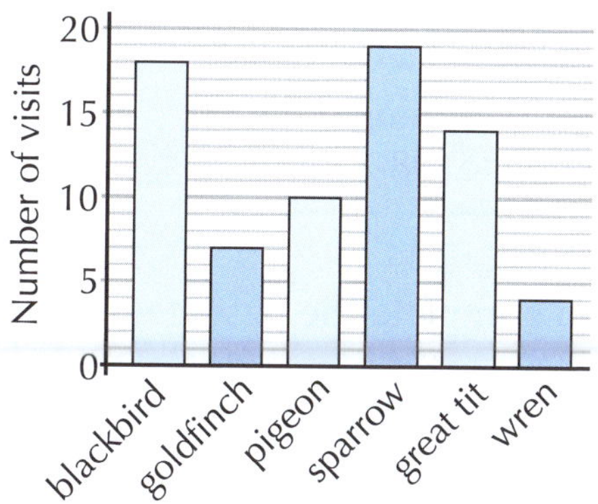

3. What is the difference between the most and fewest visits by a type of bird?

4. Aziz is putting his results into a pie chart. What will the angle of the blackbird section be? Circle the correct option.

A	20°	**C**	120°	**E**	45°
B	60°	**D**	90°		

5. Kile's train set off at 17:25. He arrives 8 hours and 40 minutes later. Which of the
following clocks shows the time he arrived? Circle the correct option.

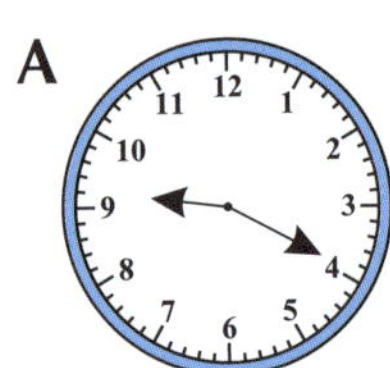 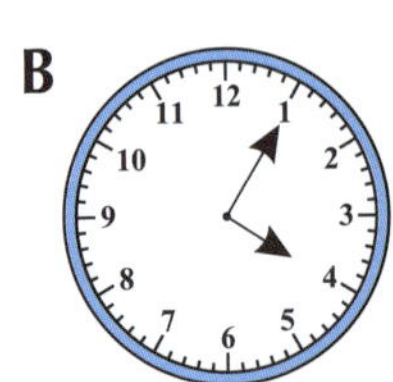 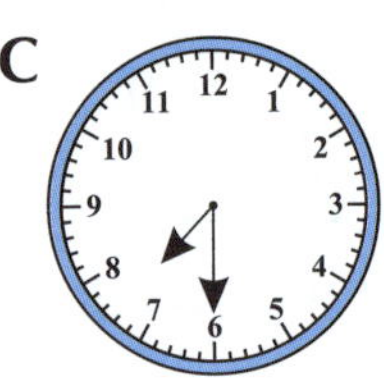 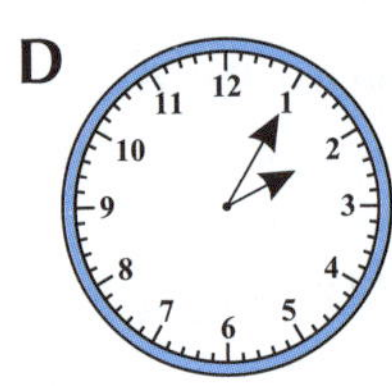 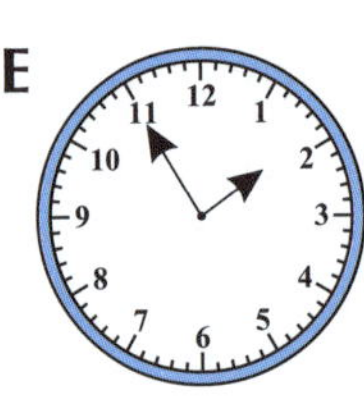

6. Nico goes fishing for two and a half hours. He catches 5 fish in the first hour,
3 fish in the second hour and 2 fish in the last half-hour.
What is the mean number of fish Nico caught per hour?

7. $4a + 3b = -24$. If $b = -12$, what is the value of a? Circle the correct option.

A 24   **C** 5   **E** 3

B 12   **D** 4

Q8-17 will test your **verbal reasoning** skills.
You have **4 minutes** to complete Q8-17.

Choose the correct words to complete the passage below.

Although pizza is now an

8. ☐ incredible
☐ overwhelmingly
☐ really
☐ typical

popular fast food, this was not

always the case.

9. ☐ Accustomed
☐ Traditional
☐ Stereotypical
☐ Establishment

pizza originates from Naples in Italy,

where the simple flat bread with tomato sauce provided poor families with a cheap and

10. ☐ nourishing
☐ enrich
☐ quenching   meal. Originally, there were two main types of pizza — the marinara,
☐ fulfilled

11. ☐ fisherman
☐ marinas
which was eaten by   ☐ sailor   , and the margherita, which was
☐ seafarers

12. ☐ supposed
☐ allegedly
☐ rumours
☐ thought

named after Queen Margherita in 1889. A margherita's ingredients (tomato, mozzarella,

13. ☐ reflection
☐ evoke
and basil) are said to   ☐ remind   the colours of the Italian national flag.
☐ signified

14. ☐ across
☐ span
After World War Two, pizza became increasingly popular   ☐ reaching   America and
☐ cover

15. ☐ sovereign
☐ individuals
several Italian emigrants opened their own   ☐ specialities   pizzerias. Today, rules put
☐ independent

16. ☐ appropriate
☐ recognised
in place to preserve Italian traditions state that an   ☐ authentic   Neapolitan pizza
☐ legitimate

17. ☐ blend
☐ kneaded
must have been   ☐ working   by hand before being baked in a special wood-fired oven.
☐ scoured

/ 17

Workout 21

Workout 22

Q1-11 will test your **non-verbal reasoning** skills.
You have **6 minutes** to complete Q1-11.

**Work out which option would look like the figure
on the left if it was reflected over the line.**

Reflect

1.  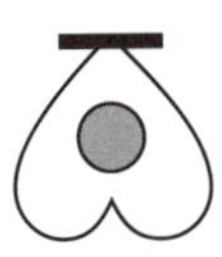 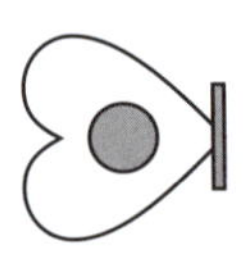 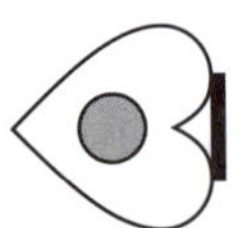 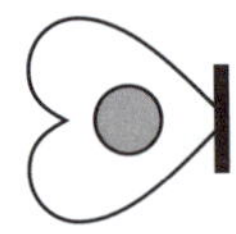

              a   b   c   d

Reflect

2.     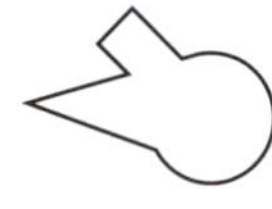

              a   b   c   d

Reflect

3. 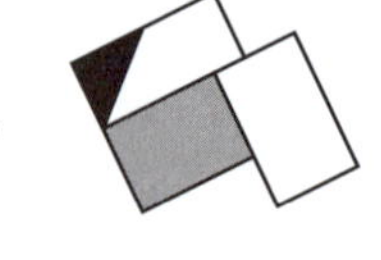 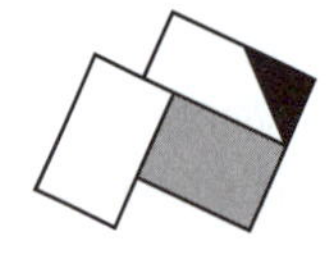 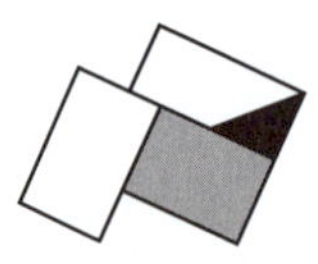  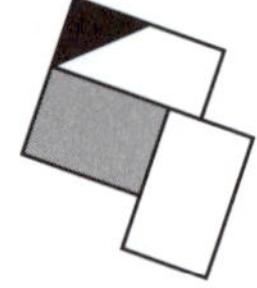

              a   b   c   d

Reflect

4.    

              a   b   c   d

Reflect

5.   

              a   b   c   d

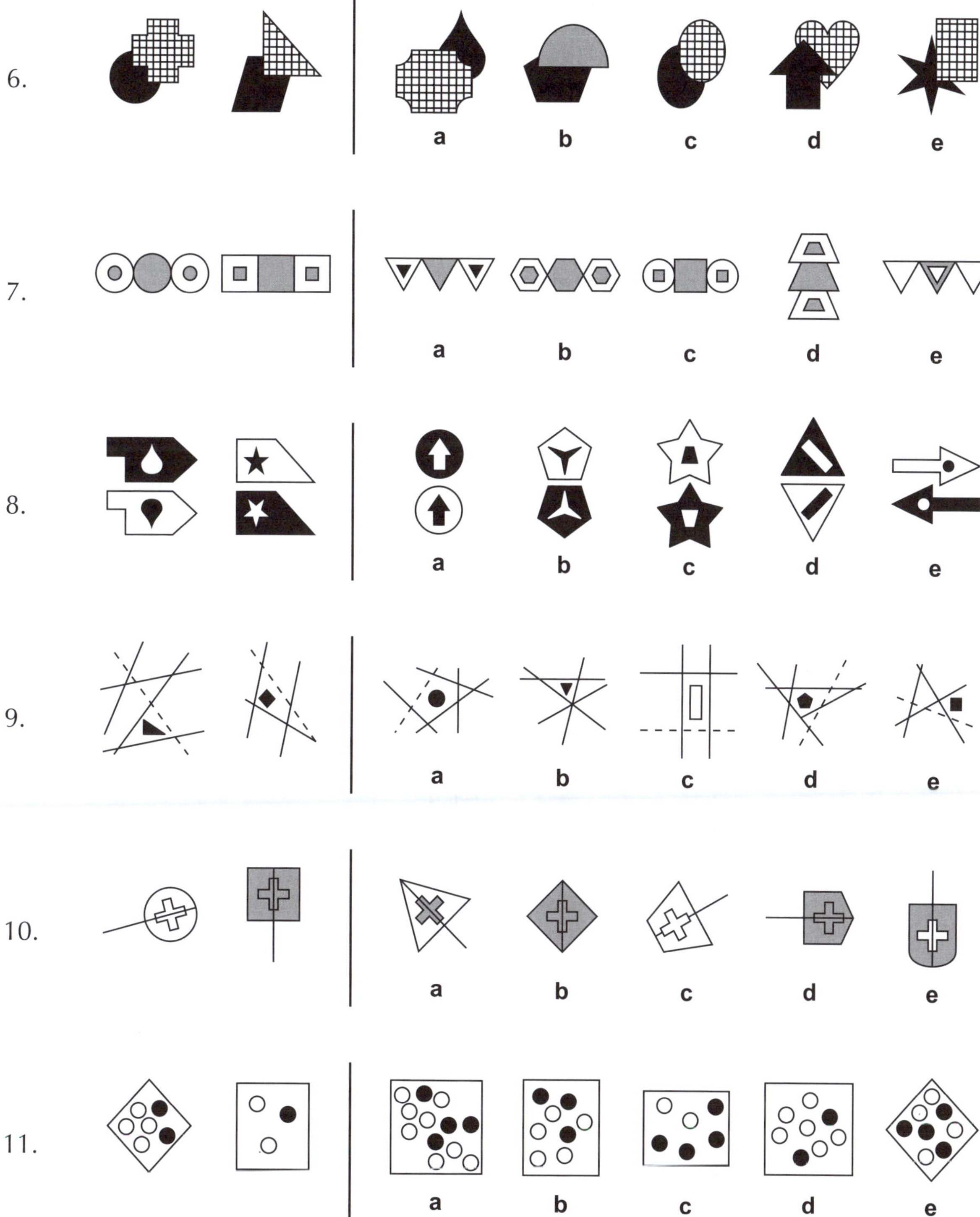

Workout 22

12. For every 2 pigs in a field there are 3 sheep.
    If there are 39 sheep in the field how many pigs are there?

13. What is the volume of the matchbox shown below?

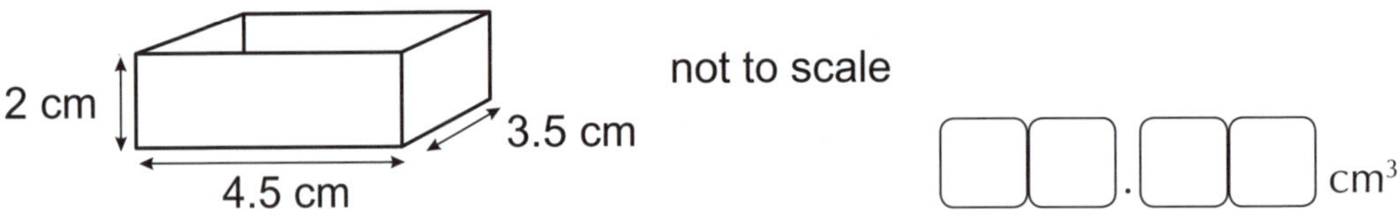

cm^3

The graphs shows how the price of a salad from a restaurant increases with the number of extra items added to the salad.

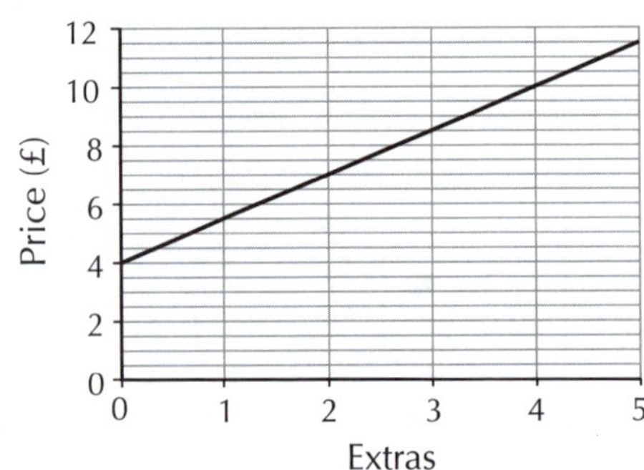

14. Gale buys one salad with 2 extras, one with 3 extras and another with
    5 extras. How much will the salads cost in total? Circle the correct option.

A £18	**C** £20.50	**E** £19
B £35.50	**D** £27	

15. The formula to calculate the price is $P = 4 + 1.5E$, where P is the price in pounds
    and E is the number of extras. How much would a salad with 7 extras be?

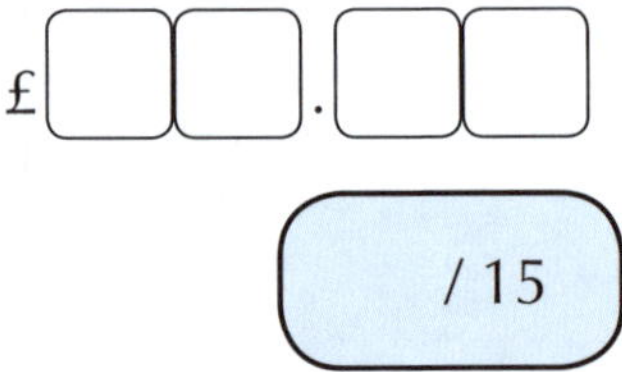

£

/ 15

Q1-11 will test your **non-verbal reasoning** skills.
You have **6 minutes** to complete Q1-11.

Look at how the first two figures are changed, and then work out which option would look like the third figure if you changed it in the same way.

1. 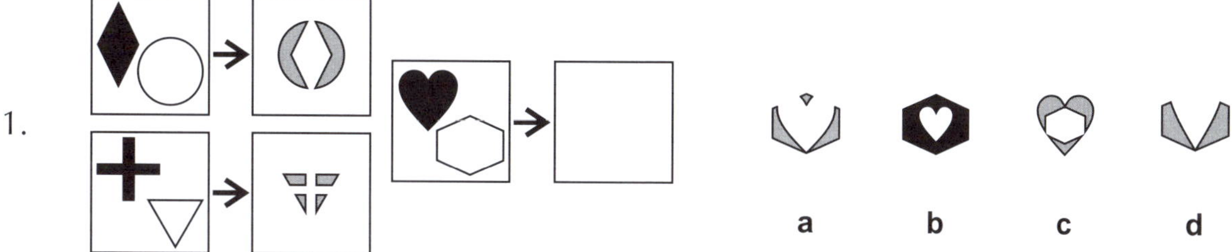

2. 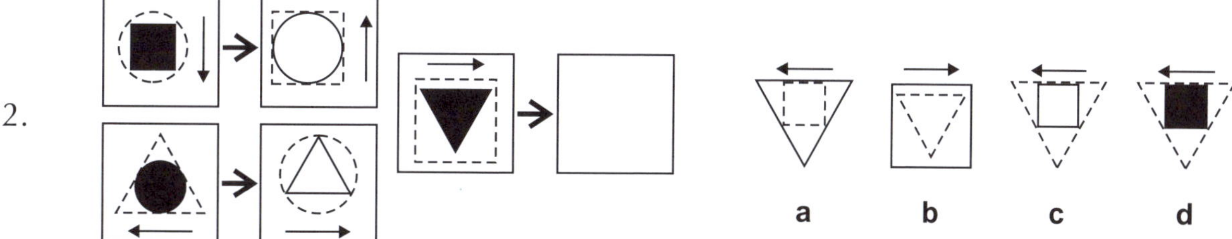

3. 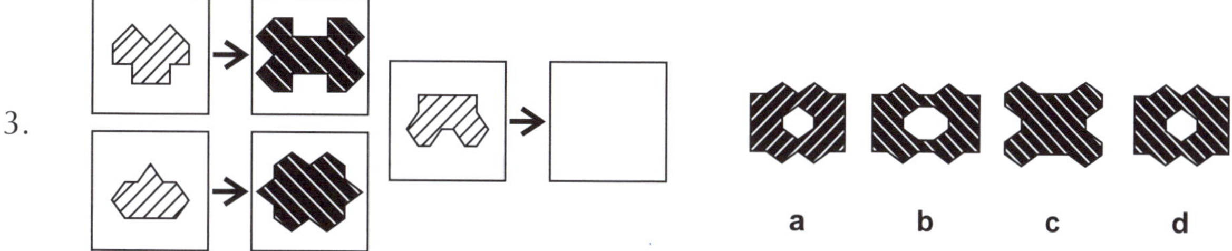

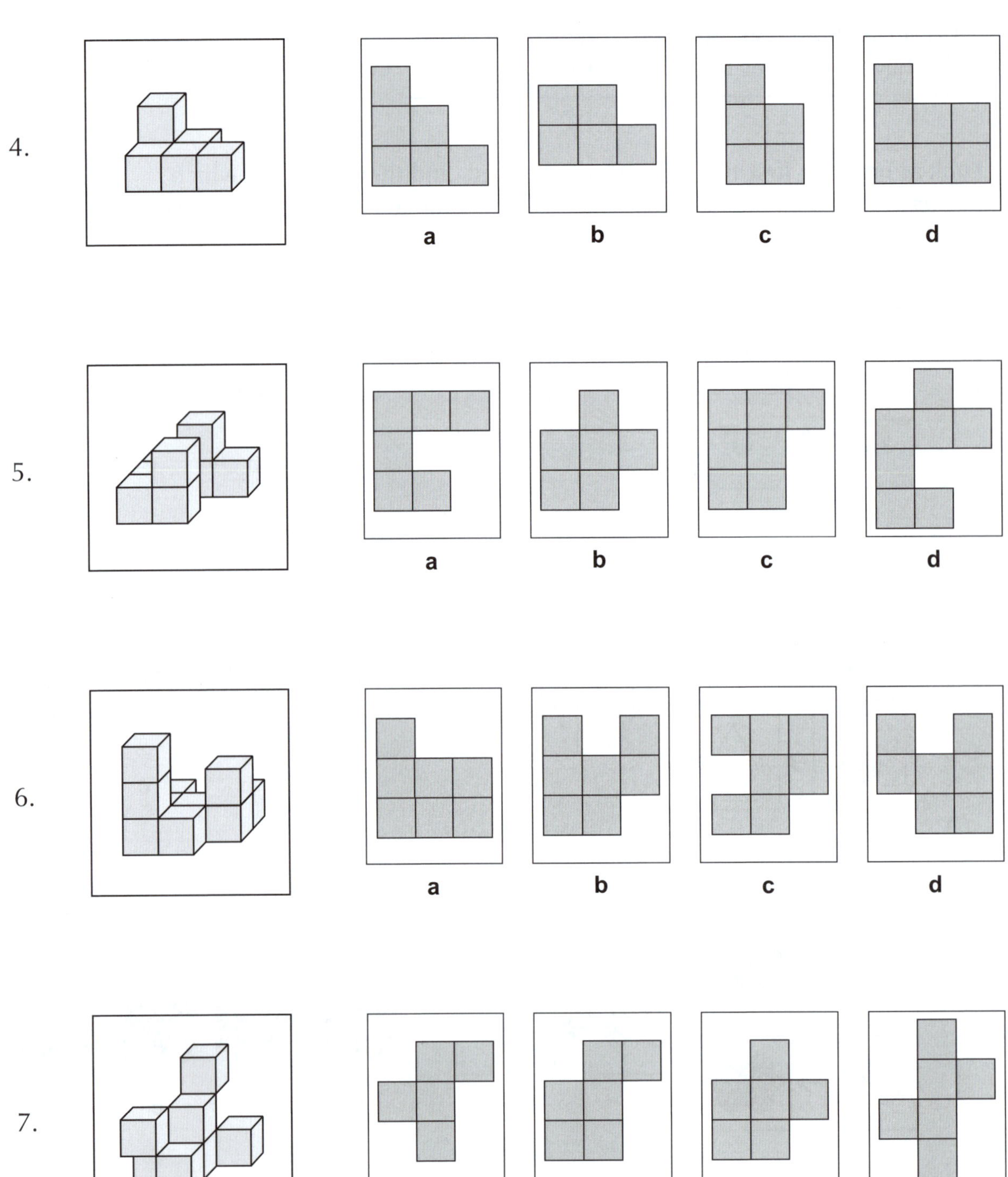

88

8. 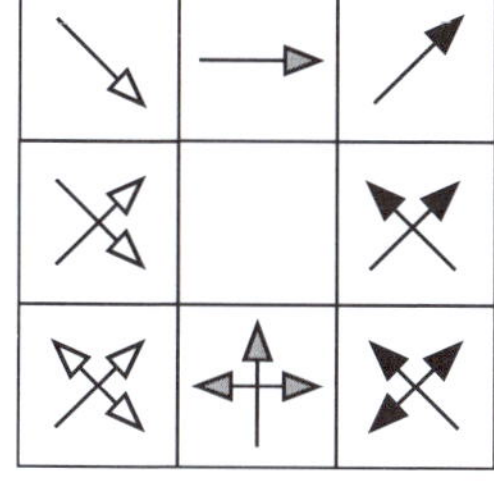
    a    b 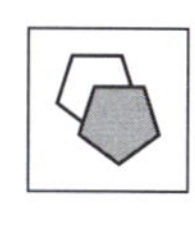   c    d    e 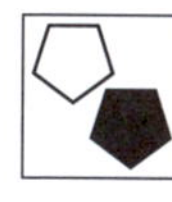

9. 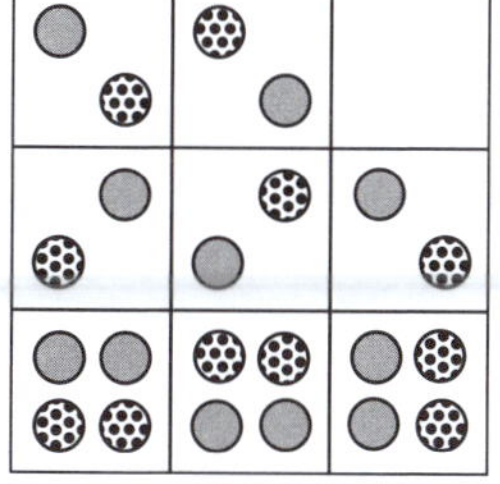
    a    b 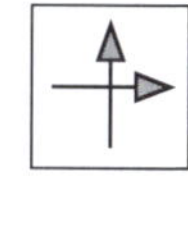   c   d   e

10. 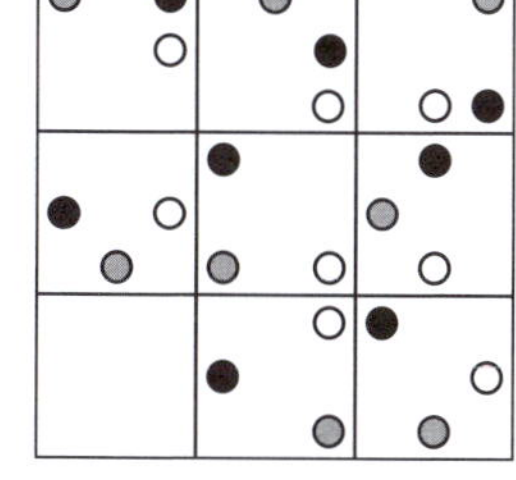
    a    b   c    d    e

11. 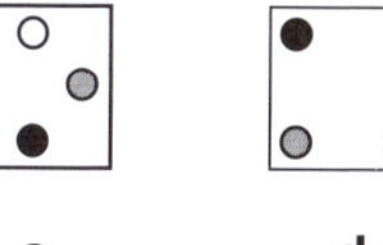
    a 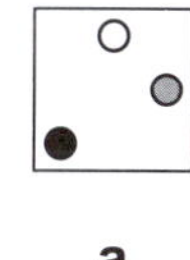   b 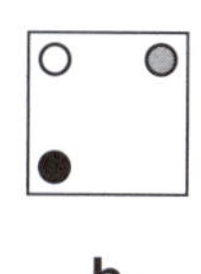   c 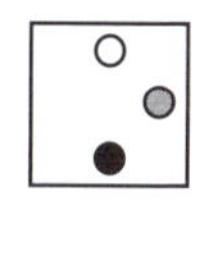   d   e 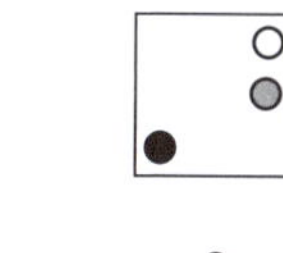

Find the word that means the same, or nearly the same, as the word on the left.

Example: **wide**   flat   straight   <u>broad</u>   long

12. **unfamiliar**   uncouth   atypical   foreign   displaced

13. **grumpy**   critical   cantankerous   threatening   exasperated

14. **seethe**   fume   soak   sulk   erupt

15. **vengeful**   envious   villainous   grudging   vindictive

16. **divergence**   deviation   isolation   desertion   progression

Complete the word on the right so that it means the opposite, or nearly the opposite, of the word on the left.

Example: heavy   [l][i][g][h][t]

17. deny   [c][ ][n][ ][ ][r][m]

18. extend   [ ][ ][t][ ][a][c][t]

19. disinterest   [b][ ][ ][ ][s]

20. blemished   [ ][l][a][ ][l][ ][ ][s]

21. construct   [d][ ][s][ ][ ][s][e][ ][b][l][e]

22. distribute   [c][ ][ ][l][ ][ ][c][ ]

23. uncertainly   [ ][ ][ ][n][f][i][ ][e][ ][t][l][y]

/ 23

Break time! These puzzles are great to practise your **angles** and **pattern-spotting** skills.

Loopy Snooker

The plan view of a parallelogram snooker table is shown on the right. When a ball hits a side, the angles it arrives and leaves at are always symmetrical — e.g:

The ball is struck and hits the top side at a 40° angle, bounces round the table and hits the top side again. Accurately draw the ball's path to find the angle it hits the top side the second time.

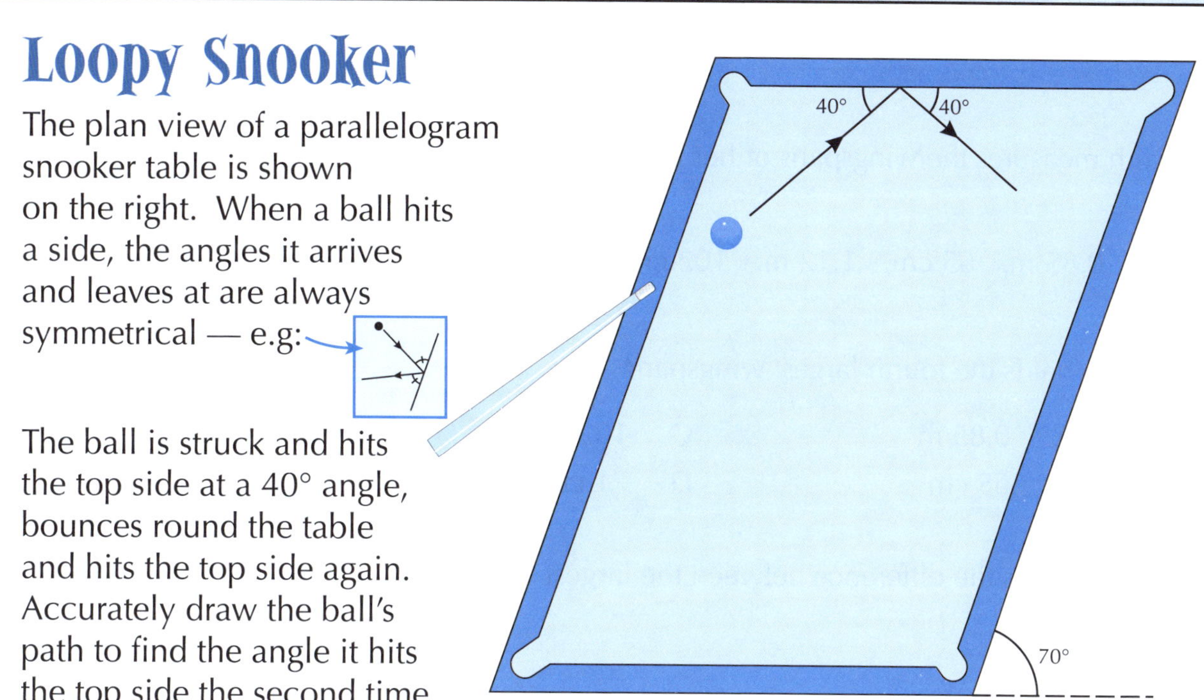

Hexagonal Havoc

Jamal made a pattern using hexagonal tiles. Hamish removed four of the tiles and mixed them up with tiles that don't fit Jamal's pattern. Find the four missing tiles.

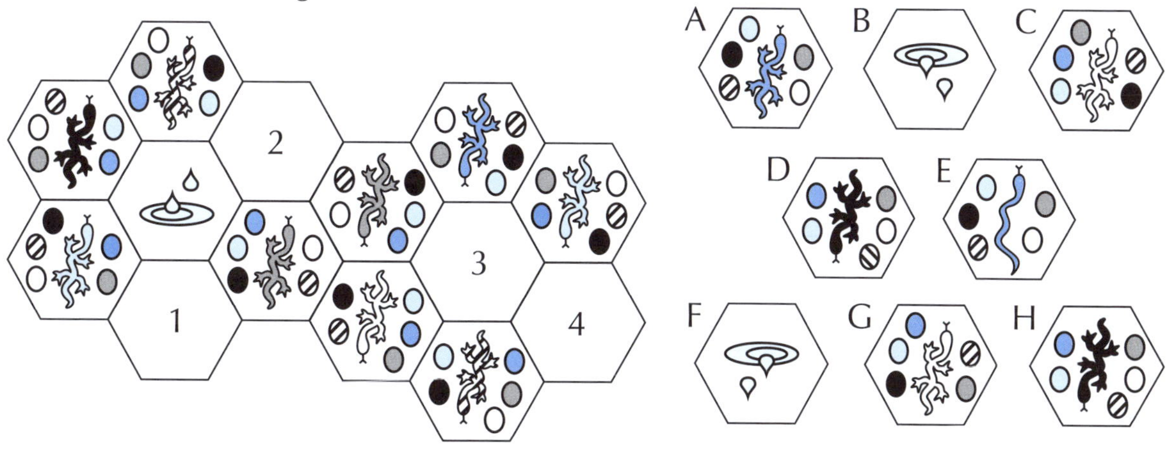

Q1-7 will test your **maths** skills.
You have **6 minutes** to complete Q1-7.

Faith measures the wingspans of her pet parrots:

0.85 m,   65 cm,   1.12 m,   102 cm,   71 cm,   73 cm,   0.5 m

1.   What is the fourth largest wingspan?

A	0.85 m	**C**	102 cm	**E**	73 cm
B	65 cm	**D**	71 cm		

2.   What is the difference between the largest and smallest wingspans?

3.   Florence is moving a shed. The grid below shows the current shaded position of
the shed and the new proposed position which is shown by the dotted outline.
How many units left and up does Florence need to move the shed?

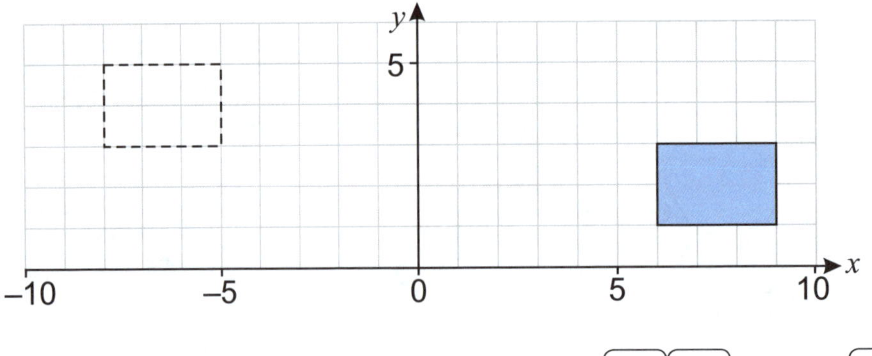

4.   What is $0.8 \div 4$?

5.   Bryony has 25 m^2 of new carpet for two rooms in her house. The sizes of the
two rooms are shown below. How much carpet will Bryony have left after
laying new carpet in both rooms?

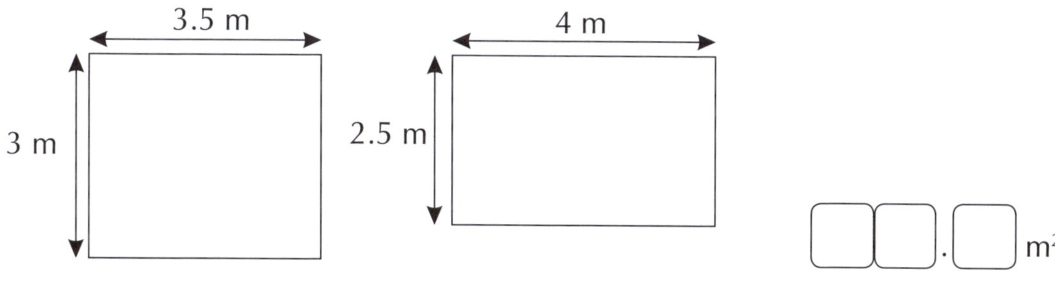

m^2

6.   Lesley has been working at a vineyard for four days. The amounts she has earned
each day form a sequence and are shown below.

$$£33, \quad £36, \quad £39, \quad £42$$

Which of the following describes how much she earns on the nth day.?
Circle the correct option.

A $30 + 3n$	**C** $30n$	**E** $3n + n$
B $10n + 3$	**D** $50 - 3n$	

7.   Felicity cuts a $\frac{1}{4}$ off from a cube of cheese. The $\frac{1}{4}$ of the cube weighs 16 g.
If 1 cm^3 of cheese weighs 1 gram, what was the height of the original cube
of cheese? Circle the correct option.

   A   3 cm

   B   16 cm

   C   8 cm

   D   4 cm

   E   2 cm

Work out which set of blocks can be put together to make the 3D figure on the left.

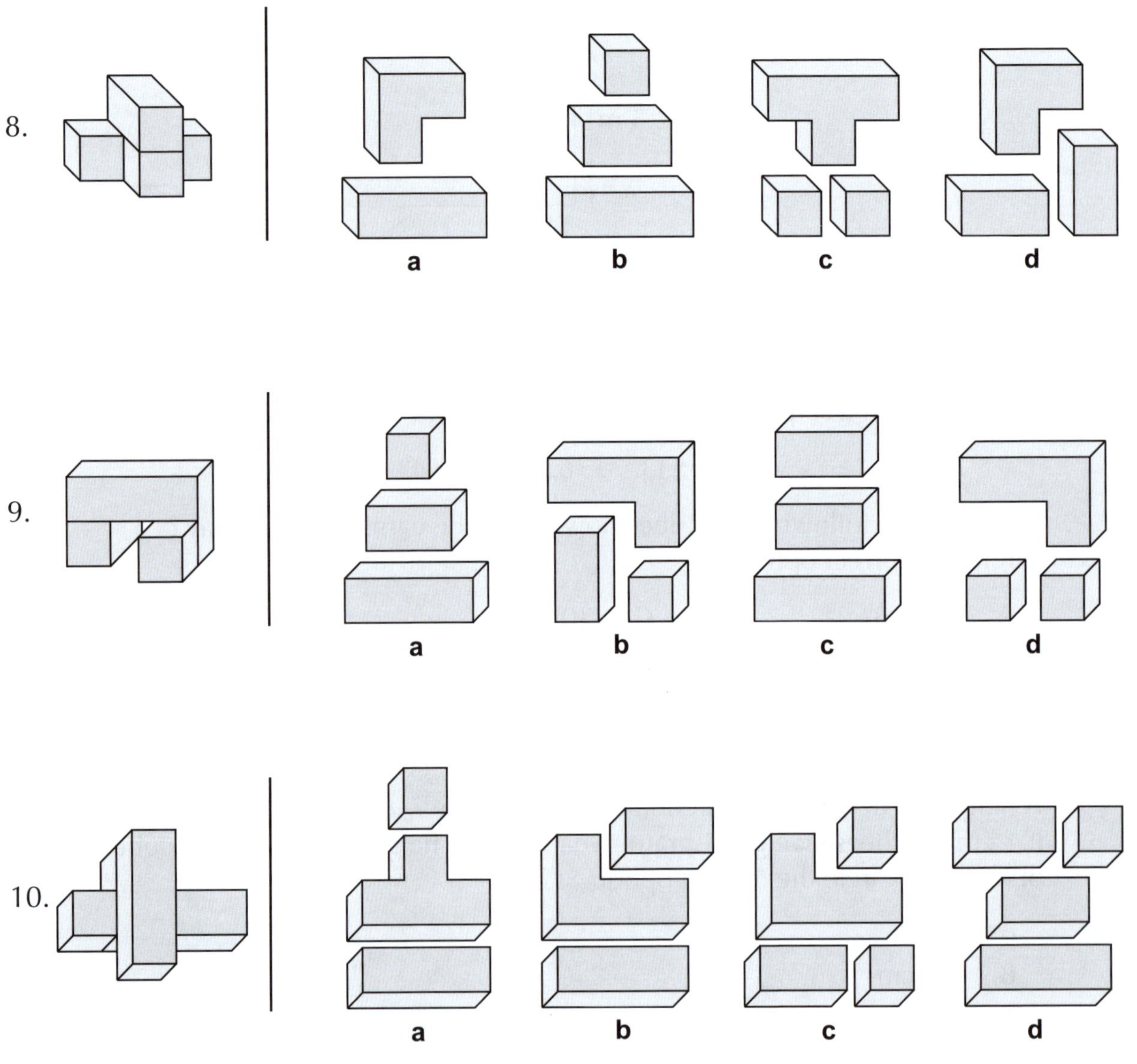

11.

12.

13.

14.

/ 14

Workout 24

Q1-10 will test your **verbal reasoning** skills.
You have **4 minutes** to complete Q1-10.

Complete the word on the right so that it means the same, or nearly the same, as the word on the left.

Example: scared a f r a i d

1. committed   d _ _ i c _ t e _

2. lament   _ _ u _ n

3. disclosure   r e _ e l _ t i _ n

4. stubborn   o _ s t _ n _ t _

5. predict   _ n t _ c _ p a _ e

Mark the word outside the brackets that has a similar meaning to the words in both sets of brackets.

Example: (twig   branch)   (fasten   attach)   glue <u>stick</u> affix bough

6. (circuit   loop)   (wash   splash)   ripple   lap   course   tour

7. (resilient   strong)   (taxing   demanding)   tough   arduous   stout   stiff

8. (flatten   demolish)   (rank   standing)   ravage   station   total   level

9. (peak   top)   (fall   topple)   crest   apex   tip   tilt

10. (bulk   capacity)   (book   tome)   edition   size   amount   volume

11. What is $5^2 - 4^2$?

12. Zubin uses 60 grams of sugar, 120 grams of butter and 180 grams of flour
     to make shortbread. What is the ratio of sugar to flour in the shortbread?
     Circle the correct option.

A	1:2	**C**	1:3	**E**	2:3
B	2:1	**D**	3:2		

13. What is $^3/_{16} + {}^3/_8$? Circle the correct option.

A	$^6/_{16}$	**C**	$^6/_8$	**E**	$^9/_8$
B	$^9/_{16}$	**D**	$^6/_{24}$		

14. The first four rectangles in a sequence are shown below.

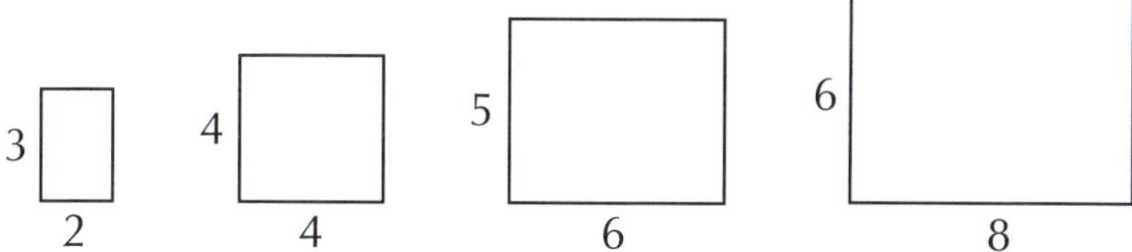

What is the area of the next rectangle in the sequence?

15. Which of the following shows the plan view of the 3D shape below?
    Circle the correct option.

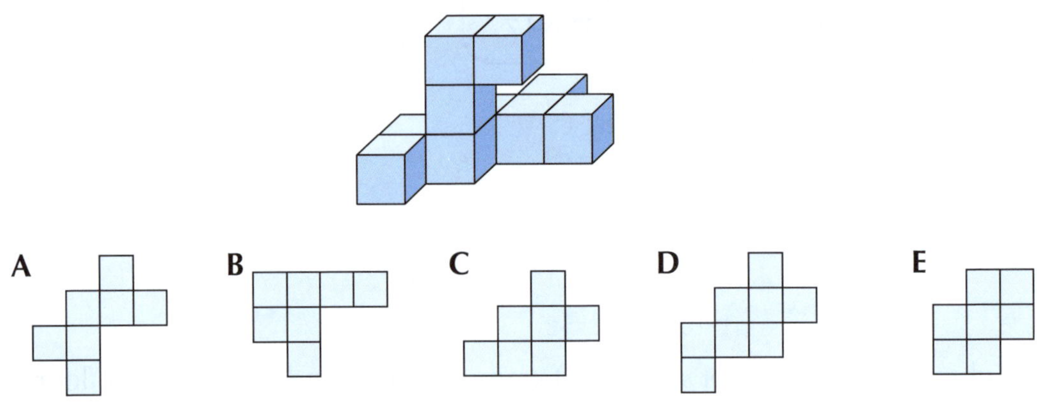

A **B** **C** **D** **E**

16. $32 \div 2a = 8$. What is the value of a?

17. Ivan and Karina are running in a sponsored charity event. The graph below
    shows how much money they raise, depending on how far they run.

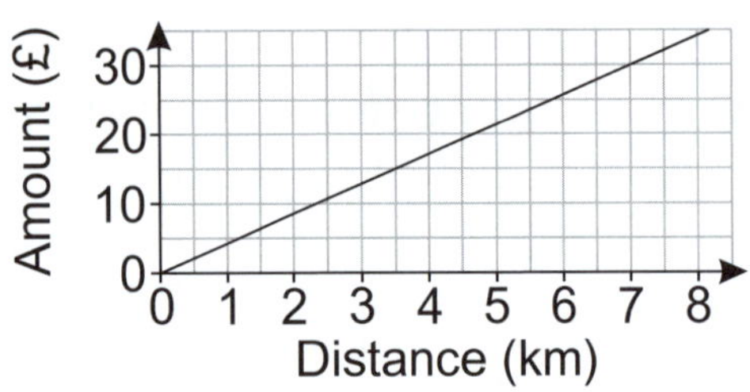

Karina runs 12.3 km. Ivan raises £45.
How much further does Karina run than Ivan?

m

/ 17

Q1-7 will test your **non-verbal reasoning** skills.
You have **4 minutes** to complete Q1-7.

Find the figure in each row that is most unlike the others.

1.    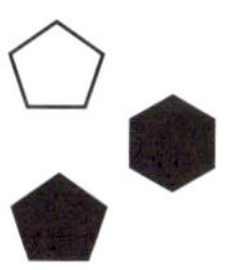 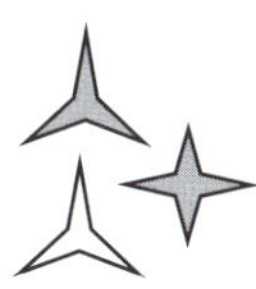

    a   b   c   d   e

2.     

    a   b   c   d   e

3.  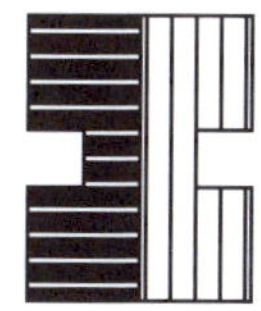   

    a   b   c   d   e

4. 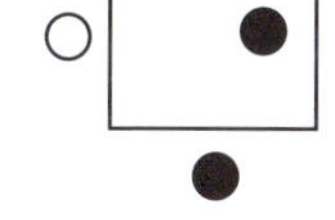 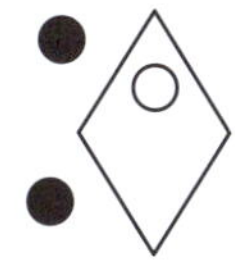 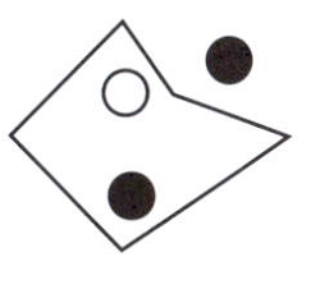 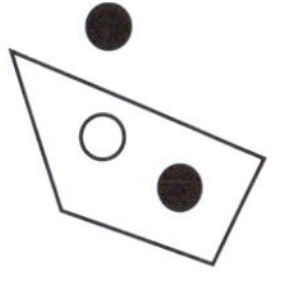 

    a   b   c   d   e

5. 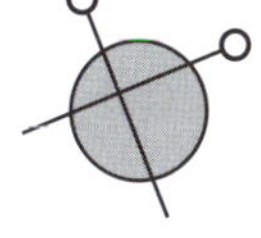 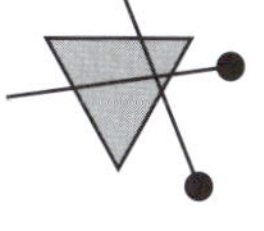 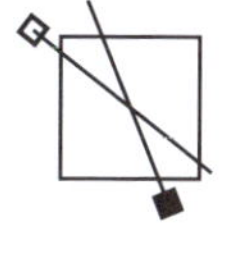 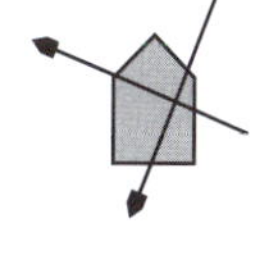 

    a   b   c   d   e

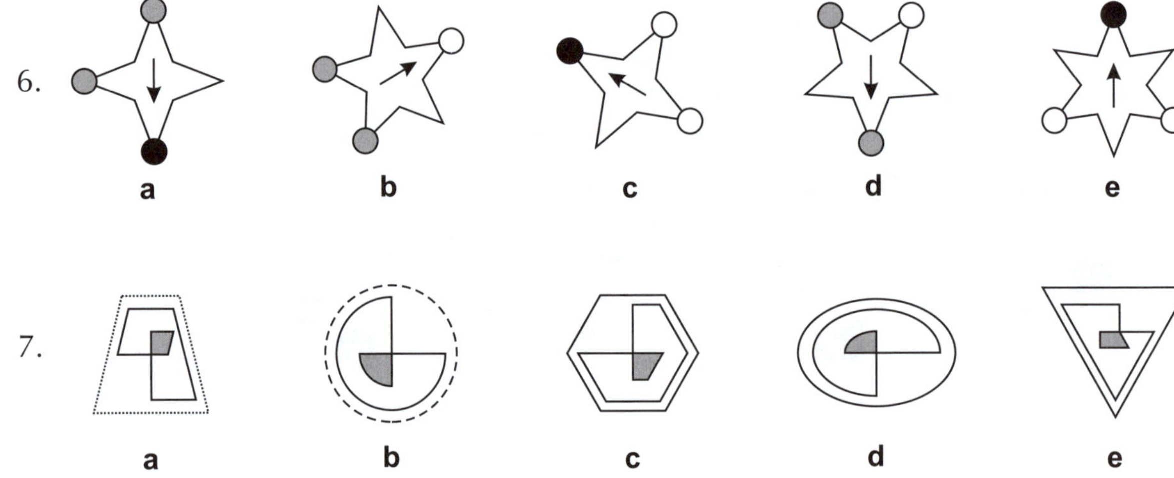

Q8-25 will test your **verbal reasoning** skills.
You have **6 minutes** to complete Q8-25.

In each question below, the words can be rearranged to form a sentence.
One word doesn't fit in the sentence. Underline the word that doesn't fit.

Example: red   the   has   <u>ride</u>   girl   bicycle   a

8.   her   weak   paper   incredibly   well   was   to   written   letter   the

9.   site   everyone   to   the   helmets   on   promised   mask   building   wear

10.   loud   up   my   wake   sirens   clock   enough   me   isn't   alarm   to

11.   younger   climbed   Katie's   was   Everest   he   failure   when   dad   Mount

12.   cheese   smelled   mouse   to   does   new   eat   our   pet   like   not

Three of the words in each list are linked. Mark the word that is not related to these three.

Example: journal   diary   <u>textbook</u>   notebook

13. lithe   sleek   silky   glossy

14. limp   hobble   stutter   shuffle

15. watch   spectacles   bracelet   bangle

16. recall   withdraw   decamp   retreat

17. wrinkle   crease   furrow   flush

18. rotate   pivot   alternate   swivel

Find the word that means the opposite, or nearly the opposite, of the word on the left.

Example: **first**   later   <u>last</u>   next   beginning

19. **lenient**   hateful   limited   temperate   severe

20. **noxious**   harmless   rejuvenating   righteous   gracious

21. **plunge**   advance   accelerate   ascend   immerse

22. **pride**   misery   humility   passivity   reticence

23. **deep**   pensive   superficial   profound   cursory

24. **official**   indecent   furtive   sanctioned   unauthorised

25. **deterioration**   alteration   regression   improvement   reawakening

/ 25

These puzzles are fantastic for practising your **vocabulary** and **problem-solving** skills.

Superior Synonyms

Romesh wants to use more exciting words to make his story more interesting. Fill in the gaps below to complete a synonym for each of the words in bold.

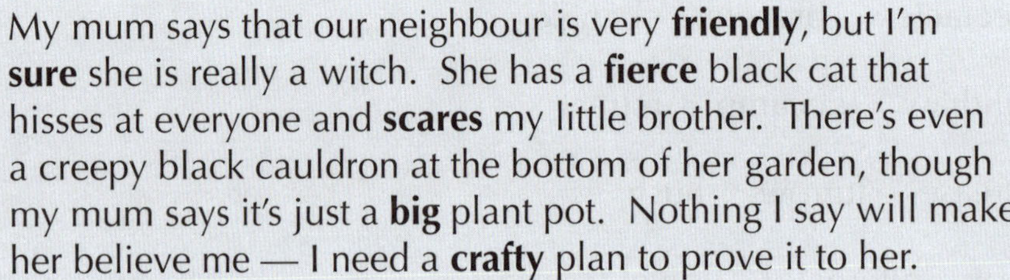

1. _ f f _ b _ _ _

2. _ _ n v i _ c _ _ _

3. f _ r _ c _ _ _ s

4. _ n t i _ i d _ t _ _ _

5. _ i _ a _ t _ c

6. _ u _ n i _ _

Mind the Cliff

Amy's hot air balloon is heading towards a cliff and is 50 m away. To get the balloon to rise, Amy can blast the burner, which makes the balloon rise by 13 m, or drop a ballast, which makes the balloon rise by 7 m.

- How can Amy make the balloon rise exactly 60 m using the burner and the ballasts?

- If the balloon travels 9 m forward every time the burner is used, how can Amy get over the height of the cliff by using only the burner?

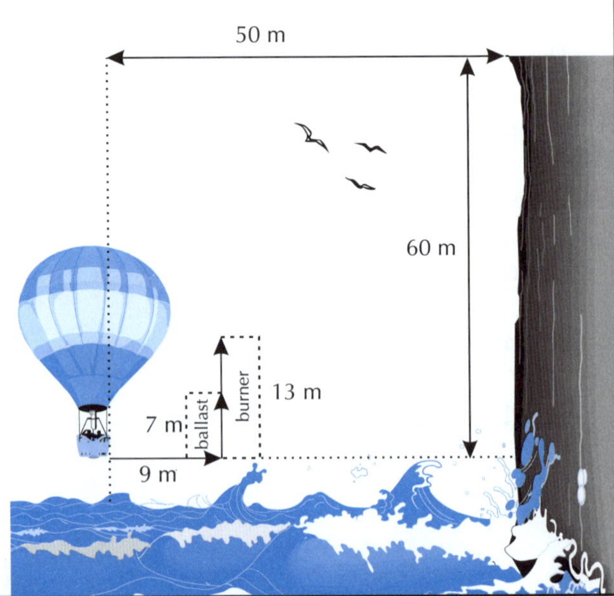

Q1-7 will test your **comprehension** skills.
You have **6 minutes** to complete Q1-7.

Read this passage carefully and answer the questions that follow.

The Brontë Sisters

Charlotte, Emily and Anne Brontë were three sisters who defied expectations for nineteenth-century women. Far from the literary circles of London, in the impoverished village of Haworth on the edge of some of Yorkshire's dramatic moorland, they wrote some of the most famous novels in the English language.

5   The sisters showed rich imagination from an early age and as children they created the elaborate fantasy worlds of 'Angria' and 'Gondal'. Their father, a clergyman, always encouraged his children's education, and they soon began writing their stories down. This sparked their ambition to become published authors.

    Their love of writing continued into adulthood, and Charlotte was determined that
10 all three of them should get their work published. They successfully found a publisher for their joint book of poetry, which they published under names that disguised their female identity — Currer, Ellis and Acton Bell. These pseudonyms corresponded to the initials of their real names. In the nineteenth century, many people considered it inappropriate for women to make a living from writing, and the Brontës feared they
15 would face prejudice if their true identities were known.

    Although their poetry only sold a handful of copies, the sisters were undeterred and strived to publish their novels. After Charlotte's first novel was rejected by publishers, 'Jane Eyre' went on to become an overwhelming success and established Charlotte as an important literary figure of her day. Some people were shocked by Emily's
20 'Wuthering Heights' because of the cruelty and violence it depicted. Similarly, Anne's 'The Tenant of Wildfell Hall' was controversial because of its harrowing themes. Today, the three women are renowned for their contribution to literature.

1. Which of the following best describes where the Brontës lived?

    A   An isolated cottage on the moors.

    B   A village on the outskirts of London.

    C   A deprived part of the country.

    D   On the border between Yorkshire and Derbyshire.

2. According to the text, what inspired the Brontës to pursue writing careers?

    A   Their father was an established author and poet.

    B   As children, they wrote stories about imaginary lands.

    C   They felt that education was very important.

    D   They found life in their village very boring.

3. Which of the following statements about Acton Bell is true?

    A   He is the youngest Brontë brother.

    B   It is the name of the publishing company that printed the sisters' poetry.

    C   It is the pen name of Anne Brontë.

    D   He is a fan of the Brontës' work.

4. Which of the following statements is true?

    A   Charlotte was jealous of Emily's poetry.

    B   The Brontës felt that writing was a childish pastime.

    C   The sisters thought that books by women were less likely to be published.

    D   Anne was reluctant to be published alongside her sisters.

5. Which of the following statements about the Brontës' careers must be false?

    A   The Brontës' collection of poetry was a commercial success.

    B   The sisters wrote prose as well as poems.

    C   Charlotte's work initially faced opposition from publishers.

    D   Charlotte was more famous than her sisters during her lifetime.

6. According to the text, what did Emily and Anne's novels have in common?

    A   They were lauded for their originality.

    B   They were criticised for using harsh language.

    C   They outsold Charlotte's 'Jane Eyre'.

    D   Their subject matter was considered inappropriate by some.

7. According to the text, which of the following statements about the Brontë sisters must be true?

    A   They overcame dire poverty.

    B   They behaved as women of their time were expected to.

    C   They were at the centre of London society.

    D   They produced influential works of literature.

> Q8-12 will test your **maths** skills.
> You have **4 minutes** to complete Q8-12.

8. Eleanor buys a mango for 80p using a £5 note. She is given her change as four pound coins and the rest in 5 pence pieces. How many 5 pence pieces does she receive?

9. Gerry cuts 9 equal lengths of wood from a 85 cm long plank. He has 4 cm left over. How long is each of the 9 lengths?

    cm

10. The diagram below shows a lake on a map. Each square of the grid is 1 km².
Use the grid to estimate the area of the lake. Circle the correct option.

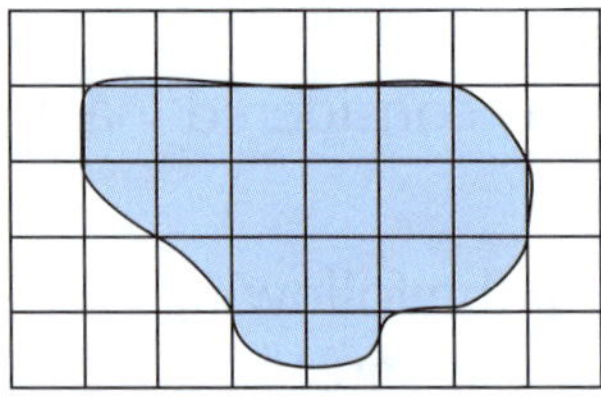

A 22 km²	**C** 25 km²	**E** 30 km²
B 18 km²	**D** 12 km²	

11. Which of the following expression is incorrect? Circle the correct option.

A $11 \times 11 = 47 + 74$

B $7 \times 12 = 14 \times 6$

C $144 \div 12 < 16 \times 1.5$

D $^{26}/_6 + {}^{10}/_6 > 50 \div 10$

E $160 - 79 = 41 \times 2$

12. Nestor rented a car for 5 days. The cost of renting the car in Euros is worked
out using the expression $30d + 2m$, where d is the number of days and m is the
number of miles over 500 driven during the rental period. Over the 5 days
Nestor drove 576 miles. How much did renting the car cost him?

€ ☐☐☐

/ 12

10

Q1-5 will test your **maths** skills.
You have **4 minutes** to complete Q1-5.

1. Victor has 25 chocolates. Every day he eats three chocolates. After how many days will he have only one chocolate left? Circle the correct option.

A 9	**C** 5	**E** 7
B 8	**D** 10	

2. The diagram shows a cross-section of a bath tub, which is a semicircle. How deep is the bath at its deepest point?

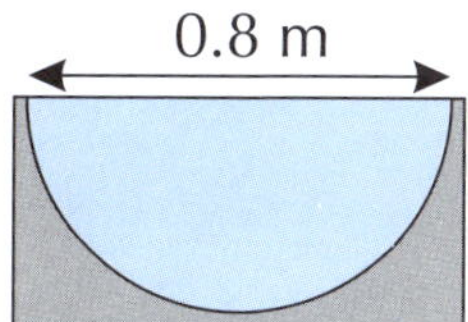

☐☐ cm

Uma recorded the number of emails she received each day for a week and the number of those which were advertising emails.

Day	Emails	Advertising Emails
Monday	25	15
Tuesday	21	
Wednesday	29	6
Thursday	18	10
Friday	34	21

3. Work out the percentage of the emails Uma received on Monday that were not advertising emails. Circle the correct option.

A 80%	**C** 60%	**E** 70%
B 20%	**D** 40%	

4. The mean number of advertising emails Uma received per day was 12.2. How many advertising emails did Uma receive on Tuesday?

☐☐

5. Donna has been on a ferris wheel for 4 minutes. The wheel takes 24 minutes to complete one full turn. How many more degrees from this point will the wheel turn through before Donna is back to where she got on?

Q6-16 will test your **non-verbal reasoning** skills. You have **6 minutes** to complete Q6-16.

Work out which option would look like the figure on the left if it was rotated.

6.  **Rotate**

a   b   c   d

7.  **Rotate**

a   b   c   d

8.  **Rotate**      

          a   **b**   **c**   **d**

9. 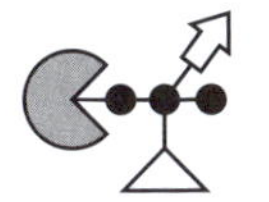 **Rotate**   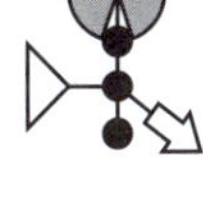 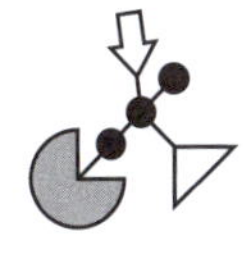 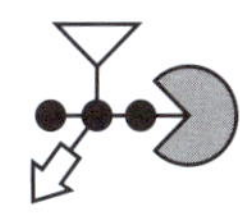

          a   **b**   **c**   **d**

10. 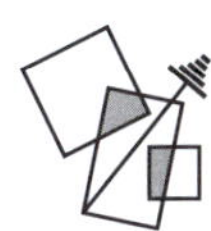 **Rotate**   

          a   **b**   **c**   **d**

Look at how the first bug changes to become the second bug. Then work out which option would look like the third bug if you changed it in the same way.

11.  :    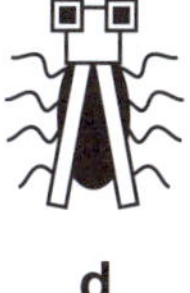

          a   **b**   **c**   **d**

12. 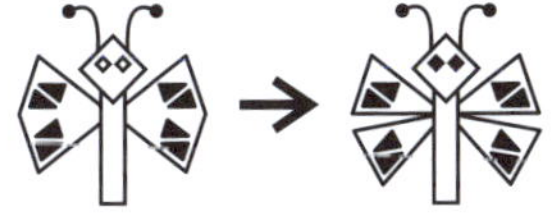 : 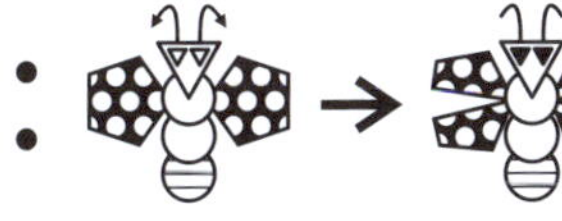 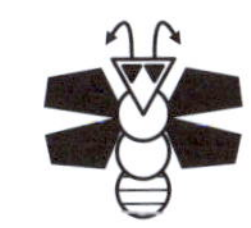  

          a   **b**   **c**   **d**

Workout 28

13. 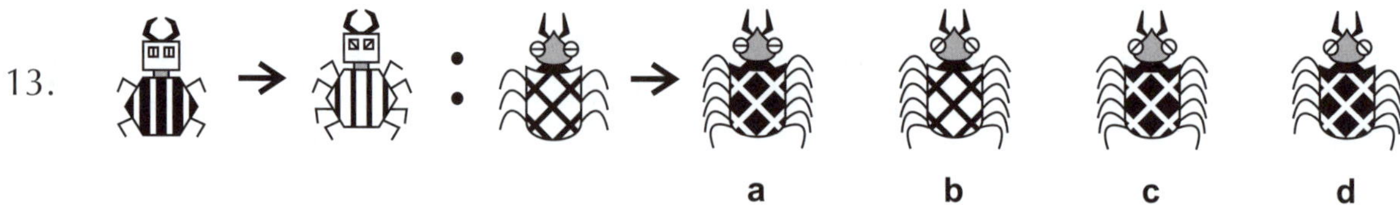

          a   b   c   d

Work out which of the options best fits in place of the missing hexagon in the grid.

14.

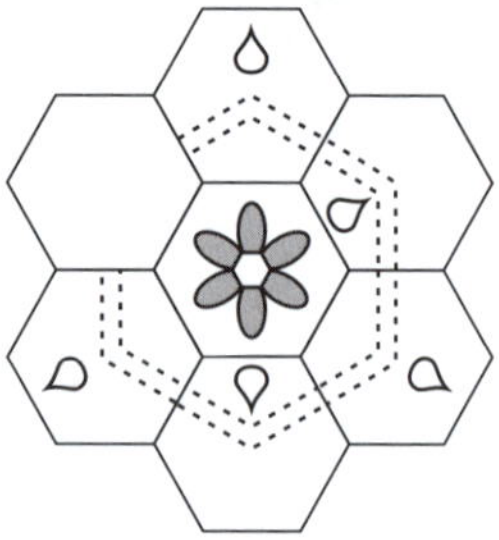

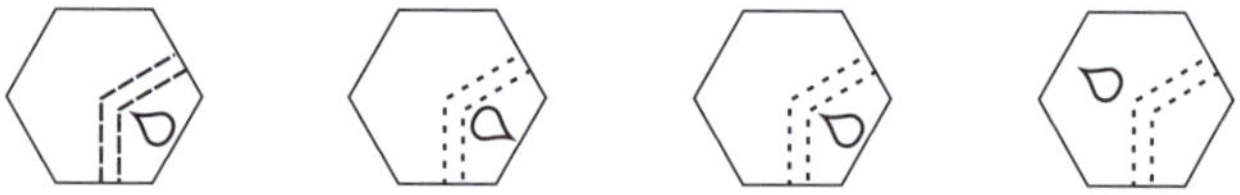

      a   b   c   d

15.

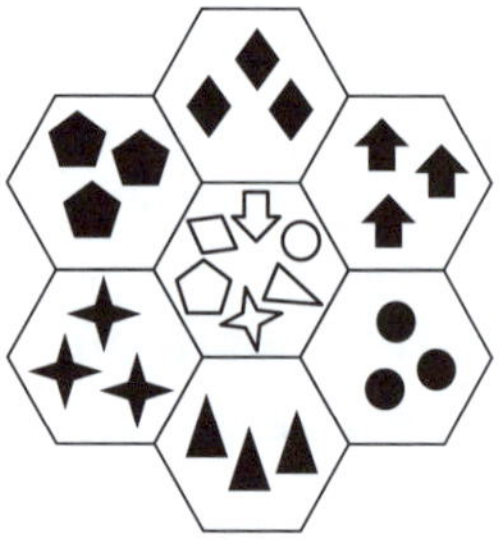

      a   b   c   d

16.

      a   b   c   d

/ 16

Q1-7 will test your **comprehension** skills.
You have **6 minutes** to complete Q1-7.

Read this passage carefully and answer the questions that follow.

An abridged extract from 'A Study in Scarlet'

We met next day as he had arranged, and inspected the rooms at No. 221B,
Baker Street. They consisted of a couple of comfortable bed-rooms and a single large
airy sitting-room, cheerfully furnished, and illuminated by two broad windows. So
desirable in every way were the apartments, and so moderate did the terms seem
5   when divided between us, that the bargain was concluded upon the spot, and we at
once entered into possession. That very evening I moved my things round from the
hotel, and on the following morning Sherlock Holmes followed me with several boxes
and portmanteaus*. For a day or two we were busily employed in unpacking and
laying out our property to the best advantage. That done, we gradually began to settle
10 down and to accommodate ourselves to our new surroundings.

Holmes was certainly not a difficult man to live with. He was quiet in his ways,
and his habits were regular. It was rare for him to be up after ten at night, and he
had invariably breakfasted and gone out before I rose in the morning. Sometimes
he spent his day at the chemical laboratory, sometimes in the dissecting-rooms, and
15 occasionally in long walks, which appeared to take him into the lowest portions of
the City**. Nothing could exceed his energy when the working fit was upon him; but
now and again a reaction would seize him, and for days on end he would lie upon the
sofa in the sitting-room, hardly uttering a word or moving a muscle from morning to
night.

20   As the weeks went by, my interest in him and my curiosity as to his aims in life,
gradually deepened and increased.

Arthur Conan Doyle

* portmanteaus — *suitcases*
** the City — *the City of London*

1. Which of the following best describes the sitting room?

    A   Dingy and uninviting

    B   Vast and lavish

    C   Comfortable and compact

    D   Bright and spacious

2. According to the text, which of the following statements must be true?

    A   The rent for the apartment is very reasonable.

    B   The apartment is close to John's hotel.

    C   John and Sherlock manage to negotiate a lower rent.

    D   Sherlock knows the owner of the apartment.

3. Which of the following words best describes how
    Sherlock and John behave in lines 1-6?

    A   Impatiently   **C**   Tentatively

    B   Decisively   **D**   Dutifully

4. Which of the following words best describes Sherlock in lines 11-13?

    A   Predictable

    B   Candid

    C   Cordial

    D   Erratic

5. What does the word "invariably" (line 13) mean?

    A   In a changeable manner

    B   In a strange manner

    C   In a consistent manner

    D   In an unpleasant manner

6. Which of the following best describes Sherlock's habits?

    A   He only frequents respectable parts of London.

    B   He spends most of his time resting.

    C   He is often out all night.

    D   He engages in scientific study.

7. According to the text, how does John feel about Sherlock?

    A   He thinks he and Sherlock are too different to live together.

    B   He admires Sherlock's lifestyle.

    C   He is intrigued by Sherlock.

    D   He thinks Sherlock is lazy.

> Q8-12 will test your **maths** skills.
> You have **4 minutes** to complete Q8-12.

8. What is $0.5 \times 4691 \times 2$?

9. Neville is putting paintbrushes into pots. Each pot can hold 11 brushes.
    How many pots will he need for 91 brushes?

10. An ice cube tray has 12 wells that make perfect identical cubes. Each well
     is 2 cm deep. What volume of water can the ice cube tray hold in total?
     Circle the correct option.

    A   100 cm^3

    B   82 cm^3

    C   96 cm^3

    D   78 cm^3

    E   50 cm^3

Seren identified 72 flying insects that she found in her garden. Her results are
shown in the pie chart below.

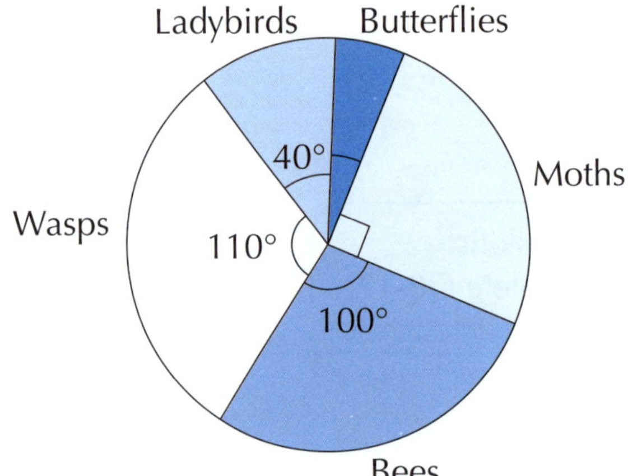

11. What fraction of the insects were either wasps or bees? Circle the correct option.

    A $^7/_{12}$ **C** $^{11}/_{16}$ **E** $^6/_{11}$

    B $^5/_6$ **D** $^1/_9$

12. Half of the butterflies Seren identified were white. How many white butterflies
     did she identify?

/ 12

Q1-7 will test your **maths** skills.
You have **6 minutes** to complete Q1-7.

1. The clock below shows the time Harper arrived home one evening.
    If it took her 1 hour and 35 minutes to get home, what time did she set off?

2. A shop is having a 20% discount sale. Helle buys a towel in the sale for £8.
    What was the price of the towel before the sale?

Gibran records the number of steps he takes each day:

7892, 12 098, 10 097, 11 204, 8981

3. What is the difference between the greatest and the fewest number of
    steps taken by Gibran on a single day?

4. Use estimation to work out the mean number of steps Gibran took per
    day. Circle the correct option.

A 11 023.4	**C** 10 054.4	**E** 13 230.6
B 88 701.2	**D** 6291.9	

5. Rory is swimming lengths of a pool. His target is 8 lengths. Rory has swum
    four and a half lengths. How much of his target has he already completed?
    Circle the correct option.

    A $\frac{1}{8}$ **C** $\frac{7}{16}$ **E** $\frac{9}{16}$

    B $\frac{3}{8}$ **D** $\frac{3}{5}$

The rectangle show on the axes below has a width of 2 units and a height of 4 units.
Point *P* on the rectangle has the coordinates $(b, 3)$.

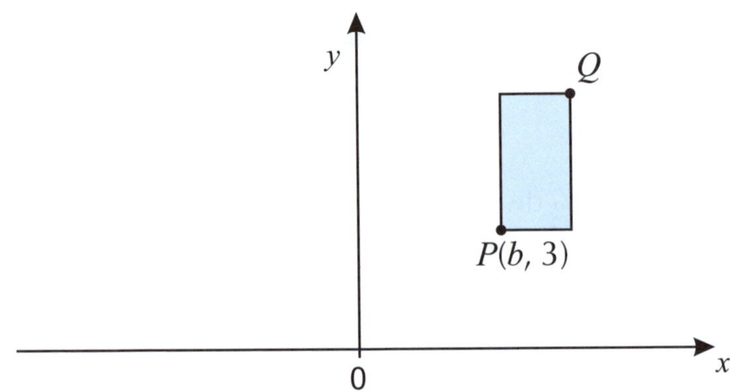

6. Which of the following describes the coordinates of point *Q*?
    Circle the correct option.

    A $(2, 3)$ **C** $(2b, 3)$ **E** $(-b - 2, 7)$

    B $(-2, 3)$ **D** $(b + 2, 7)$

7. The rectangle is moved so that the new coordinates of *P* are $(-b, 2)$.
    Which of the following describes how the rectangle was moved?
    Circle the correct option.

    A 1 right and $3b$ up

    B b right and b up

    C $2b$ left and 1 down

    D $2b$ right and 2 up

    E 2 left and 2 up

Look at how the first two figures are changed, and then work out which option would look like the third figure if you changed it in the same way.

8.

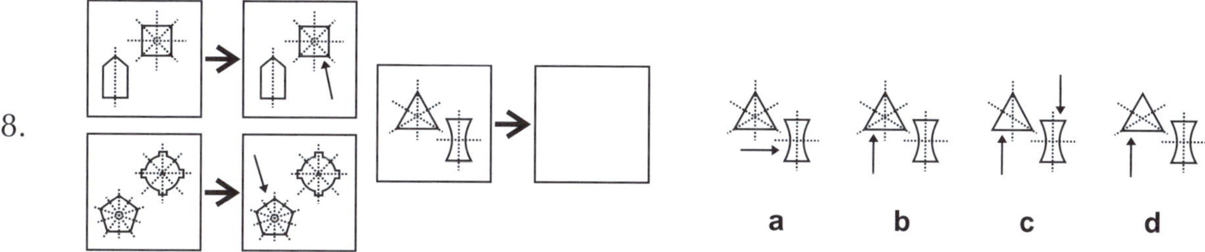

9.

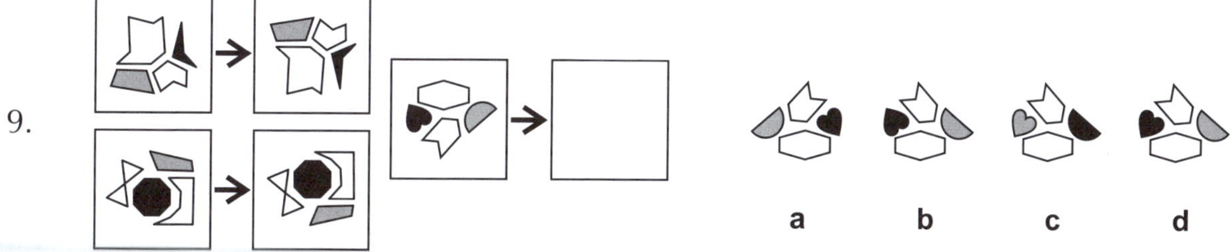

10.

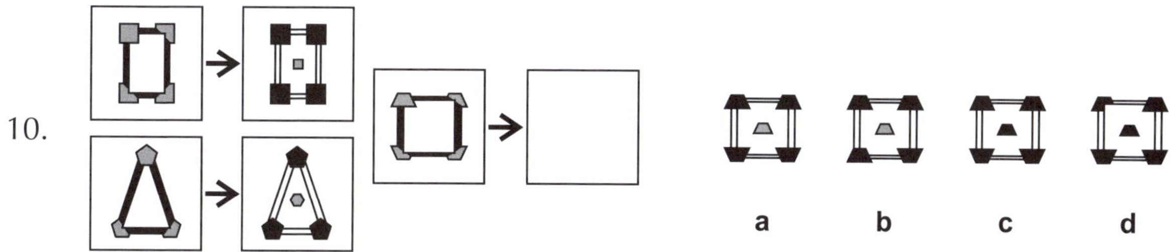

Work out which 3D figure in the grey box has been rotated to make the new 3D figure.

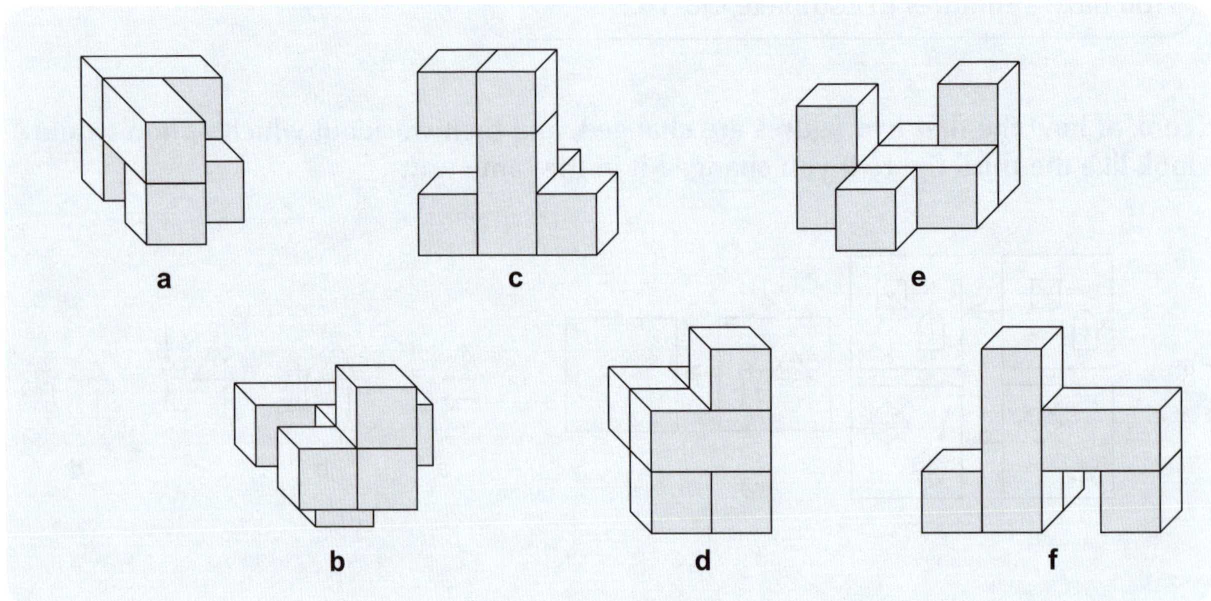

a   c   e

b   d   f

11.

a	d
b	e
c	f

12. 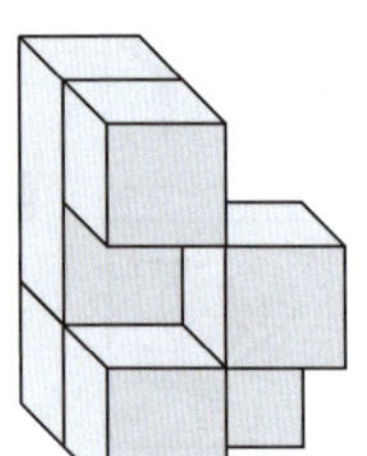

a	d
b	e
c	f

13.

a	d
b	e
c	f

14. 

a	d
b	e
c	f

/ 14

CGP

11+

Mixed Workouts

Ages 10-11

The 10-Minute Test Answer Book

Book 1

Mixed Workouts

For the CEM (Durham University) test

Practise • Prepare • Pass

Everything your child needs for 11+ success

L6XWDE1

Workout 1 — pages 2-5

1.   A
Subtract 11 from 4 °C : 4 – 11 = –7. So it's –7 °C today.

2.   14:12
At 14:00 the cake has been in for 23 minutes.
35 – 23 = 12, so it needs another 12 minutes
after 14:00, which is 14:12.

3.   (8, 8)
Point a is 3 squares away from the line, so its
reflection will also be three squares away from it,
but on the other side of the line. This is (8, 8).

4.   C
You find each term by adding $^2/_3$ to the previous
term. So the next term will be $2\,^1/_3 + ^2/_3 = 3$.

5.   70%
There are 30 days in April. $^{21}/_{30}$ simplifies down to $^7/_{10}$
(divide both numbers by 3), which is the same as 70%.

6.   10 cm
Five presents need 50 cm of ribbon: 5 × 50 = 250 cm.
Three presents need 80 cm: 3 × 80 = 240 cm.
So the total length of ribbon needed is
250 + 240 = 490 cm. Franklin started with 5 m
which is 500 cm, so 500 – 490 = 10 cm.

7.   E
The hexagon is regular and O is the centre point so x is one
sixth of 360°. 360 ÷ 6 = 60°. So the side length is
$2x = 2 × 60 = 120$ cm. Then the perimeter of the hexagon
is 6 × 120 = 720 cm, which is the same as 7.2 m.

8.   B
Each hexagon is reflected across the
middle of the hexagonal grid.

9.   D
Going in a clockwise direction around the hexagonal
grid, the pattern rotates 60 degrees clockwise
each time. The shading of the circle inside the
triangle alternates between black and white.

10.   B
The hexagons on opposite sides of the
hexagonal grid are identical.

11.   A
Going around the hexagonal grid, each hexagon is reflected
over the line joining it to the next hexagon. The eight-
sided shapes swap shadings after each reflection.

12.   B
There are six blocks visible from above, which rules out
options A and C. There are only three blocks visible
on the left-hand side, which rules out option D.

13.   C
There are six blocks visible from above, which rules
out option B. There are two blocks visible at the
front, which rules out options A and D.

14.   A
There are seven blocks visible from above, which rules
out option D. There are three blocks visible at the front,
which rules out option B. There are two blocks visible
on the right-hand side, which rules out option C.

Workout 2 — pages 6-9

1.   C
Lines 3-4 state that Lamarr invented "a device
that paved the way for Wi-Fi®, Bluetooth® and
GPS technology". "paved the way for" means
her invention made future work easier.

2.   B
Lines 6-7 state that Lamarr "was described as the
most beautiful woman in the world", and line 8 states
that "She was renowned for her glamour and looks".

3.   B
Lines 9-10 state that Lamarr had a "lack of
formal scientific training", meaning that she
had no official training in science. However, she
"studied and became knowledgeable about"
science, suggesting that she taught herself.

4.   D
Line 12 states that she "identified a flaw in the US Navy's
torpedoes", and lines 14-15 state that she "designed a
guidance system for torpedoes" which corrected this flaw.

5.   C
Line 13 states that the torpedoes "could be sent
off course if the radio signals were interfered with",
suggesting that the enemy could interfere with them.

6.   A
Lines 15-16 state that the Navy "appropriated Lamarr
and Antheil's ideas". "appropriated" means 'took without
permission'. Lines 16-17 state that their work "remained
unacknowledged for decades", which means their work
wasn't recognised.

7.   C
Lines 18-20 state that it "wasn't until the 1990s"
that Lamarr's work was "recognised", after which she
"was honoured with awards by the scientific community"
for "Her pioneering work in radio communication".

8.   D
There are four lines of symmetry:

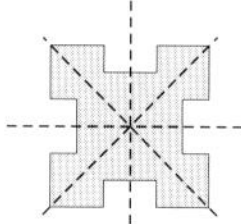

9.   144
$6^2 = 6 × 6 = 36$, and 72 – 68 = 4. So you need
to do 36 × 4. You can use partitioning here:
36 = 30 + 6. 4 × 30 = 120, and 4 × 6 = 24.
So 36 × 4 = 120 + 24 = 144.

10.   18 cm²
The shape is made of a rectangle and a triangle — the base
of the triangle is 6 – 2 = 4 cm, and its height is 5 – 2 = 3 cm:

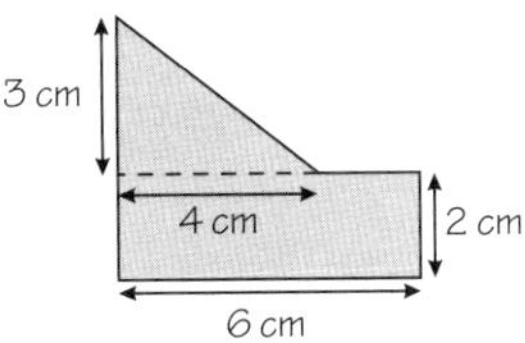

The rectangle has area 6 × 2 = 12 cm².
and the triangle has area $^1/_2$ × 4 × 3 = $^1/_2$ × 12 = 6 cm².
So the total area is 12 + 6 = 18 cm².

11.   C
The angles of a triangle add up to 180°.
So x + a + 4a = 180. This can be simplified
to x + 5a = 180, which if you take 5a from
both sides you get x = 180 – 5a.

12.   30°
Put a = 30° into the equation from Question 11:
x = 180 – 5 × 30 = 180 – 150 = 30°.

Puzzles 1 — page 10

Alien Antics
B

Cooking Crisis
The ingredients are: PARSNIPS, TOMATOES, CUSTARD,
ORANGES, GARLIC, BISCUITS
The final ingredient is **CARROTS**.

Workout 3 — pages 11-14

1.   C
The figure rotates 90 degrees clockwise.

2.   B
The shading of the shape changes and a smaller, identical
shape appears inside it. The smaller shape has the
same shading that the large shape used to have.

3.   B
The cross increases in size and moves into the middle
of the figure. The white shape becomes black.

4.   D
An arrow appears, pointing to the largest shape in the figure.

5.   D
Option A is ruled out because the circle and the square
must be on opposite sides. Option B is ruled out
because there is no black square on the net. Option
C is ruled out because the black triangles and one of
the black semicircles must be on opposite sides.

6.   B
Option A is ruled out because if the white drop is at the
front and the black lines are on the top, then the black
and white circles should be on the right. Option C is ruled
out because the pentagon and the black lines must be on
opposite sides. Option D is ruled out because the black
and white circles and the star must be on opposite sides.

7.   C
Option A is ruled out because the black triangle should point
away from the white square. Option B is ruled out because
if the white square is at the front and the white triangle is
on the top, then the star should be on the right. Option D is
ruled out because the triangles must be on opposite sides.

8.   B
Option A is ruled out because the line and diamond figure
should be pointing away from the arrow. Option C is ruled
out because if the grey shape is at the front and the black
circles are on the top, then the line and diamond figure
should be on the right. Option D is ruled out because if the
black bar is at the front and the grey shape is on the top,
then the square should be on the right.

9.   B
Working from left to right, the small shape from the
figure in the left-hand column appears without the
large shape in the middle column. Then the large
shape from the figure loses a side and appears
without the small shape in the right-hand column.

10.   D
The figures in each column are identical except
for the shading of the shape at the front. Each
shading of the shape at the front exactly
appears once in each row and column.

11.   C
Working from left to right, the shape in the bottom
right-hand corner of each grid square rotates 90
degrees clockwise. The shadings move one place
clockwise around the shapes in each grid square.

12.   before
The words can be rearranged into the sentence
'You must obtain a licence in order to drive cars.'

13.   exercise
The words can be rearranged into the sentence
'We went out walking and got caught in a storm.'

14.   working
The words can be rearranged into the sentence
'Several plumbers arrived to fix the flooded bathroom.'

15.   ball
The words can be rearranged into the sentence
'Chuckles the clown did not like wearing his red nose.'

16.   slip
The words can be rearranged into the sentence
'A hole in my fence allowed three sheep to escape.'

17.   vision
The words can be rearranged into the sentence
'Eating carrots helps you to see in the dark.'

18.   moist
'arid' means 'dry', whereas 'moist' means 'damp'.

19.   flustered
'calm' means 'undisturbed', whereas
'flustered' means 'agitated'.

20.   wane
'increase' can mean 'to get more intense',
whereas 'wane' means 'to lessen'.

21. deceit

'honesty' means 'truthfulness', whereas
'deceit' means 'dishonesty'.

22. euphoria

'depression' can mean 'extreme sadness', whereas
'euphoria' means 'extreme happiness'.

23. altruistic

'selfish' means 'self-centred', whereas
'altruistic' means 'selfless'.

Workout 4 — pages 15-17

1. A

The figure is rotated 90 degrees anticlockwise.
In option B, the lines have the wrong shading. In option C,
the thinner line has the wrong shading. In option D,
the lines are in the wrong place.

2. D

The figure is rotated 90 degrees clockwise.
Option A is a downwards reflection. In option B, the
square has the wrong rotation. In option C, the square
and the circle have swapped positions and shadings.

3. C

The figure is rotated 135 degrees clockwise. In option A,
the shape in the middle is wrong. In option B, the shapes
on the ends of the dashed line are wrong. In option D,
the shape in the middle has the wrong rotation.

4. C

The figure is rotated 90 degrees clockwise. Option A is a
rotated reflection. Options B and D are the wrong shape.

5. B

The figure is rotated 180 degrees. In option A, the
small black circle and white square have swapped
places. In option C, the white arrow has the wrong
rotation. Option D is a rotated reflection.

6. C

All figures must have a shape at the top which has been
reflected downwards. The hatching of the top shape must
be rotated 45 degrees anticlockwise in the bottom shape.

7. D

In all figures, the arrows must be running along
a pair of parallel sides of the shape.

8. C

All figures must have two smaller versions of the large
shape on the outer ellipse. The shading of the small shapes
must be different to the shading of the large shape.

9. A

All figures must have two solid lines
and one dashed line. The shapes on
either end of the black stripe must be different.

10. E

In all figures, the number of sides on each
shape increases along the arrow.

11. B

In all figures, the shading of the shapes in the
stack alternates between black and white.

12. 57 000

You're rounding to the nearest thousand so you have
to look at the digit in the hundreds column. It's 7, so
you round the thousands digit up to give 57 000.

13. 53 889

2824 people leave, so subtract 2824 from 56 713:

$$
\begin{array}{r}
5\,6\,7\,1\,3 \\
-\ \ 2\,8\,2\,4 \\
\hline
5\,3\,8\,8\,9
\end{array}
$$

14. D

To find the 18th term replace n with 18 in the nth term
expression. $3(18 + 5) = 3(23) = 3 \times 23 = 69$.

15. 36

The sector for pink is 90°. The sector for blue is 180°,
so $a = 180° \div 6 = 30°$. This means the sector for
yellow is 30°. $b = 360° - 180 - 90 - 30 = 60°$, so the
sector for green is 60°. $^{60}/_{360} = {}^{1}/_{6}$, so $^{1}/_{6}$ of the
pencil cases sold were green. 216 pencil cases were
sold so $^{1}/_{6}$ of 216 is $216 \div 6 = 36$ pencil cases.

Workout 5 — pages 18-21

1. tradition — 'its **tradition** of masks.'

2. souvenirs — 'Popular with today's
tourists as **souvenirs**'

3. associated — 'widely **associated** with'

4. opportunity — 'an **opportunity** for revellers'

5. ornately — 'masks are **ornately** decorated'

6. stark — 'others are a **stark** white.'

7. sinister — 'the **sinister** *Medico della peste*'

8. measure — 'a protective **measure**'

9. substances — 'Sweet-smelling **substances**'

10. contained — 'flowers were **contained** within'

11. D

Going in an anticlockwise direction around the hexagonal
grid, each hexagon rotates 60 degrees anticlockwise.
The arrows on opposite sides of the hexagonal grid
have the same number of small shapes at their end.

12. C

Going in a clockwise direction from the top hexagon,
the arrows and the circle swap position. The
grey circle gets bigger in each hexagon.

13. B

Shapes on opposite sides of the hexagonal grid
alternate between being the large outer shape and
the small inner shape. The shading of the shapes
around the grid alternates between white and grey.

14. A

All shapes which are shaded black or white move
into the space where the two circles overlap.

15. B

The figure breaks up into smaller white shapes.

4

16.   D
The figure is rotated 180 degrees. The shapes which make
up the figure are combined and the shading of the figure
becomes hatched with vertical and horizontal lines.

17.   B
The figure is reflected across. The grey shapes are
then reflected back to their original orientation.

18.   B
The bottom block in B is at the back of the figure.
The top block in B is at the front of the figure.

19.   D
The top block in D is on the left-hand side of the
figure. The bottom block in D is at the back of the
figure. The other two blocks in D are arranged on
the top of and on the front right of the figure.

20.   D
The top block in D is at the back of the figure. The middle
block in D is underneath it on the right. The other two blocks
in D are arranged at the front of the figure.

21.   C
The top left block in C is at the back of the figure
on the left-hand side. The bottom right block in C
is rotated to form the block on the bottom right of
the figure. The other two blocks in C are arranged on
the top right and on the front left of the figure.

Puzzles 2 — page 22

Prime Ribs
Group of 11 — 3 benches (5 + 3 + 3 or 7 + 2 + 2)
Group of 18 — 4 benches (7 + 7 + 2 + 2, 5 + 5 + 5 + 3 or
7 + 5 + 3 + 3)
The smallest group needing more than four benches is 25
— they would need 5 benches (e.g. 7 + 7 + 5 + 3 + 3).

Jungle Jump!
north

Workout 6 — pages 23-25

1.   74 minutes
11:54 to 12:00 is 6 minutes, 12:00 to 13:00 is
60 minutes and 13:00 to 13:08 is 8 minutes.
So the total time is 6 + 60 + 8 = 74 minutes.

2.   D
Work out the time between each stop — Hallow to Wilt
is 33 minutes, Wilt to Clawson is 19 minutes
and Clawson to Bardgrove is 22 minutes.
So the shortest time is 19 minutes.

3.   B
10% is the same as $^1/_{10}$. $^1/_{10}$ of 240 is 24. So, 20%
is 2 × 24 = 48. Ruben has spent 20% so you need to
subtract £48 from £240. 240 − 48 = £192.

4.   8 cm
You know that 3 × 6 × h = 144, so 18 × h = 144,
which means the height is 144 ÷ 18.
You can use partitioning on the division here:
18 = 2 × 9. 144 ÷ 2 = 72, and 72 ÷ 9 = 8,
so the height of the cuboid is 8 cm.

5.   1
The total number of cars Alessandro sees is
80 + 60 + 40 + 30 + 90 = 300. He was recording
cars for 5 hours: 5 × 60 = 300 minutes.
So the mean number of cars per minute is
300 cars ÷ 300 minutes = 1 car per minute.

6.   bright
The other three mean 'to give off light'.

7.   mallet
The other three mean 'to strike'.

8.   report
The other three are forms of electronic communication.

9.   water
The other three mean 'to extract fluid'.

10.   alpine
The other three are adjectives relating to animals.

11.   track
'track' can mean 'a path' or 'to follow closely'.

12.   dark
'dark' can mean 'grim' or 'immoral'.

13.   train
'train' can mean 'a procession' or 'to teach'.

14.   slow
'slow' can mean 'to reduce speed' or 'without haste'.

15.   appreciate
'appreciate' can mean 'to comprehend' or 'to value highly'.

16.   close
'close' can mean 'having an affectionate connection
with someone' or 'the conclusion of something'.

17.   mundane
Both words mean 'dull'.

18.   interrogate
Both words mean 'to question someone'.

19.   gratitude
Both words mean 'appreciation'.

20.   rejection
Both words mean 'refusal'.

21.   resolute
Both words mean 'strong-willed'.

22.   essential
Both words mean 'necessary'.

23.   adequate
Both words mean 'acceptable'.

Workout 7 — pages 26-29

1.   B
Line 2 states that the door is "storm-pelted",
which suggests rain is being blown against the door.

2.   C
Lines 2-4 state that the congregation gave the man
"a quick regardful eyeing", which makes the narrator realise
that "this fine old man was the chaplain", Father Mapple.

3.   B

Lines 6-7 state that Father Mapple "had dedicated his life to the Church" for "many years past".

4.   C

Lines 8-10 state that Father Mapple's "hat ran down with melting sleet" and his jacket is heavy with "the weight of the water it had absorbed". This shows his clothes are very wet.

5.   A

'lofty' and 'elevated' both mean 'high up'.

6.   D

Lines 13-14 state that "regular stairs" would "seriously contract the already small area of the chapel". This suggests that a ladder was built instead of stairs in order to save space.

7.   A

Line 18 states that Father Mapple climbs with "a truly sailor-like but still reverential dexterity". "dexterity" means 'nimbleness', and "sailor-like" also suggests that he climbs easily. "reverential" means 'showing deep respect', which makes Father Mapple seem serious and dignified.

8.   B

In each series square, the dashes in the outline of the diamond become shorter.

9.   B

In each series square, the trapezium rotates 90 degrees clockwise. The shading of the circles alternates between black and hatched.

10.   D

In each series square, the shading of the triangles rotates anticlockwise.

11.   C

In each series square, one segment from the group of two rotates clockwise to join the single segment.

12.   D

In each series square, the shapes move anticlockwise around the corners of the series square. The circles become squares and the squares become circles.

13.   B

In each series square, the number of sides of both shapes increases by two. The shading of the shapes alternates between black with white spots and white with black spots.

14.   A

In each series square, the shapes move one place up, and the top shape moves to the bottom. The position of the shading in each series square remains the same.

Workout 8 — page 30-32

1.   A

Option B has squares on each end, which will not form a pentagonal prism. Option E has hexagons on each end so that won't either. Option D has four rectangular faces — you need five to form a pentagonal prism. Option C has one pentagonal face in the wrong position. So it must be option A.

2.   5 cm

Put the heights in order from tallest to shortest: 1.85 m, 120 cm, 1.15 m, 0.9 m, 90 cm. The 2nd tallest is 120 cm and the 3rd tallest is 1.15 m, which is 115 cm. So the difference is 120 − 115 = 5 cm.

3.   1.2 m

Convert all the heights in m to cm and add them up: 120 + 90 + 115 + 185 + 90 = 600 cm. Divide 600 by the number of plants, 5. You can use partitioning here: 600 = 500 + 100. 500 ÷ 5 = 100 and 100 ÷ 5 = 20, so 600 ÷ 5 = 100 + 20 = 120 cm, which is 1.2 m.

4.   D

3.5 km is 3500 m. Rohima only has 780 m left, so subtract 780 from 3500. 3500 − 780 = 2720 m, which is the same as 2.72 km.

5.   3 minutes 15 seconds

Rohima runs 4 metres per second for 780 m. So, this takes her 780 ÷ 4 = 195 seconds, which is the same as 3 minutes and 15 seconds.

6.   A

Shape A has been rotated 90 degrees left-to-right.

7.   E

Shape E has been rotated 90 degrees right-to-left.

8.   B

Shape B has been rotated 90 degrees anticlockwise in the plane of the page.

9.   F

Shape F has been rotated 90 degrees left-to-right. It has then been rotated 90 degrees towards you, top-to-bottom.

10.   C

Shape C has been rotated 90 degrees anticlockwise in the plane of the page. It has then been rotated 180 degrees left-to-right.

11.   D

Shape D has been rotated 90 degrees left-to-right. It has then been roated 90 degrees towards you, top-to-bottom.

12.   D

All figures must have a shape with double the number of smaller shapes inside it as it has sides.

13.   E

All figures must consist of one circle, four teardrops and one triangle.

14.   C

In all figures, the shapes inside the circles must match the shape at the bottom of the figure. The shading of all the shapes must be the same.

15.   D

In all figures, the white shape must be a 90 degree clockwise rotation of the black shape. The white shape must contain half of the black shape in its original orientation.

16.   E

All figures must contain seven circles and have a diagonal line of symmetry from the top-left to the bottom-right of the figure.

Puzzles 3 — page 33

Scaly Surprise
Two times — on the first use of the scale Harriet puts three eggs on each side of the balance. One side will be heavier than the other so she knows one of those three eggs is the crocodile egg. Now she takes two of these three eggs and puts one on each side of the balance. If one is heavier then it's the crocodile egg. If the scales balance then the crocodile egg is the third egg that she didn't put back on the scales.

Antonym Actions
resist — **surrender**   divide — **combine**   continue — **quit**
facilitate — **obstruct**   expand — **shrink**   clean — **stain**
heed — **ignore**

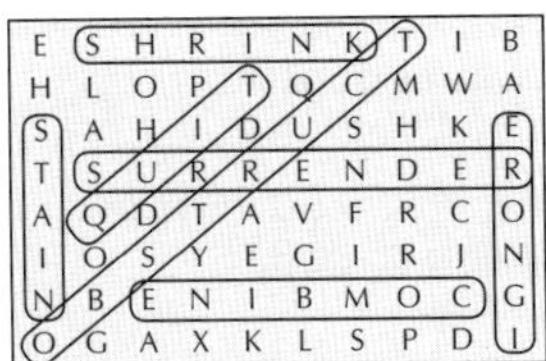

Workout 9 — pages 34-36

1.   7
4 appears only once, 5 and 8 appear twice, 6 appears three times and 7 appears four times, so 7 is the most common age.

2.   A
$^1/_4$ is equivalent to $^2/_8$,
so $^1/_4 + ^3/_8 = ^2/_8 + ^3/_8 = ^5/_8$.

3.   D
Use partitioning to multiply 115 by 7:
$115 = 100 + 10 + 5$. $7 \times 100 = 700$, $7 \times 10 = 70$ and $7 \times 5 = 35$. So $115 \times 7 = 700 + 70 + 35 = 805$ m.

4.   72°
Both pentagons are regular so they both have angles of 108°. So $2x = 360 - (2 \times 108) = 360 - 216 = 144$. This means $x = 144 \div 2 = 72°$.

5.   A
$y = 52 \div 13 = 4$, so $y^3 = 4^3 = 4 \times 4 \times 4 = 16 \times 4 = 64$.

6.   17
You need to work out how many cars started each race. Race 1 has $3^3/_4$ steering wheels so there are $3^3/_4 \times 4 = 15$ cars in Race 1 (you can work this out using partitioning). Race 2 has 5 steering wheels so $5 \times 4 = 20$ cars started. Race 3 has 4 steering wheels so $4 \times 4 = 16$ cars started. The total number of cars starting the races is $15 + 20 + 16 = 51$. So the mean number of cars per race is 51 cars $\div$ 3 races = 17 cars per race.

7.   45%
20 cars started the race and 9 cars finished it.
$^9/_{20}$ is equivalent to $^{45}/_{100}$, which is equivalent to 45%.

8.   14 cm²
The area of the original triangle would have been $^1/_2 \times 8 \times 4 = 16$ cm². The smaller triangle that was cut off has height 2 cm and base $8 - 6 = 2$ cm. So its area was $^1/_2 \times 2 \times 2 = 2$ cm². So the area of the new shape is $16 - 2 = 14$ cm².

9.   burgeon
Both words mean 'to grow rapidly'.

10.   nourishment
Both words mean 'food'.

11.   aloof
Both words mean 'distant'.

12.   quarry
Both words can mean 'a thing that is being pursued'.

13.   afterwards
Both words mean 'later on'.

14.   pillage
Both words can mean 'to steal and cause destruction'.

15.   serene
'agitated' means 'flustered', whereas 'serene' means 'calm'.

16.   poverty
'affluence' means 'wealth', whereas 'poverty' means 'not having enough money'.

17.   exhausted
'replenished' means 'restocked', whereas 'exhausted' means 'used up'.

18.   carelessly
'heedfully' means 'carefully', whereas 'carelessly' means 'without care'.

19.   haphazard
'organised' means 'ordered', whereas 'haphazard' means 'without order'.

Workout 10 — pages 37-40

1.   roamed — 'dinosaurs **roamed** Earth.'

2.   study — 'scientists who **study** dinosaurs'

3.   excavated — 'a wealth of **excavated** fossils'

4.   perennial — 'A **perennial** favourite'

5.   enthusiasts — 'many dinosaur **enthusiasts**'

6.   iconic — 'with its **iconic** horns'

7.   in — 'frequently portrayed **in** films'

8.   Contrary — '**Contrary** to what you might expect'

9.   descendants — 'thought to be **descendants** of'

10.   formidable — 'the **formidable** Tyrannosaurus Rex'

11.   E
In all other figures, there are three identical shapes in a line.

12.   D
In all other figures, the number of lines is the same as the number of points on the star.

13.   C
In all other figures, the arrow is pointing to the shape with different shading.

14.   C
All other figures have only triangles and lines.

15.   E
All other figures have the same order of shading, from left-to-right, on the small shapes.

16.   C

Each grey arrow points away from the straight side of the semicircle. Each black arrow points towards the curved side of the semicircle.

17.   B

Each shape only appears once in each row and column. The hatching in each column points in the same direction.

18.   E

The grid has a vertical line of symmetry.

19.   D

Working from left to right, the figure is rotated 90 degrees anticlockwise.

20.   E

Working from left to right, the figure in the first grid square and the figure in the second grid square are added together to make the figure in the third grid square. Each figure in the left-hand column is shaded black.

21.   A

Working from top to bottom, each figure is reflected horizontally, then it is reflected vertically.

Puzzles 4 — page 41

Clothing Catastrophe

T-shirt F is the new design. All solid lines become dashed and all dashed lines become solid. Dark blue shapes become light blue. All grey circles disappear. All small white shapes become grey.

Word Storm

The words are: **storm**, **clouds**, **forecast**, **temperature**, **showers**

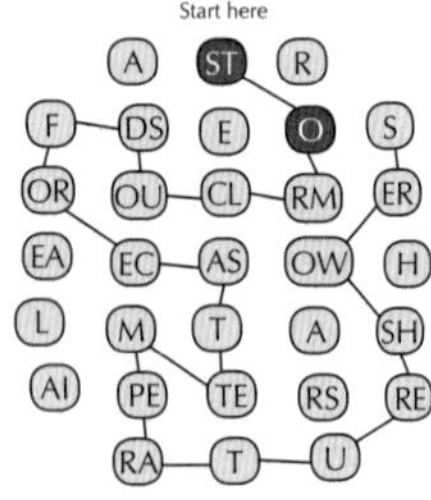

Workout 11 — pages 42-45

1.   C

There are six blocks visible from above, which rules out options A and B. There are three blocks visible on the left-hand side, which rules out option D.

2.   A

There are six blocks visible from above, which rules out option B. There is only one block visible at the back, which rules out option C. There is only one block visible at the front of the figure, which rules out option D.

3.   C

There are six blocks visible from above, which rules out option A. There is only one block visible on the left-hand side of the figure, which rules out options B and D.

4.   D

There are six blocks visible from above, which rules out option A. There is only one block visible on the left-hand side, which rules out options B and C.

5.   B

There are two blocks visible on the left-hand side of the figure, which rules out options C and D. There are two blocks visible at the back of the figure, which rules out option A.

6.   D

There are two blocks visible at the back of the figure, which rules out option B. There are two blocks visible on the left-hand side, which rules out option C. There is one block visible at the front, which rules out option A.

7.   A

There are five blocks visible from above, which rules out option C. There are two blocks visible on the left-hand side, which rules out options B and D.

8.   D

1218×52 can be estimated by $1200 \times 50 = 60\,000$. The only option close to that value is $63\,336$.

9.   14

3 'parts' of the ratio are knives. $21 \div 3 = 7$, so each 'part' is 7 knives. Forks make up 2 'parts' of the ratio. $2 \times 7 = 14$, so there are 14 forks in the drawer.

10.   £201

£33.50 is $^1/_6$ of the price so use partitioning to multiply by 6 to find the full price: $33.5 \times 6 = 180 + 18 + 3 = £201$.

11.   B

M starts at $(1, 4)$, moving 2 right and 3 down gives new coordinates of $(3, 1)$. N starts at $(5, 9)$ and moves 2 right and 3 down giving new coordinates of $(7, 6)$.

12.   2158

$215.8 \times 3.6 + 6.4 \times 215.8$ is the same as $215.8 \times (3.6 + 6.4)$, which is $215.8 \times 10 = 2158$.

13.   £11.00

Break up the lawn into two rectangles.

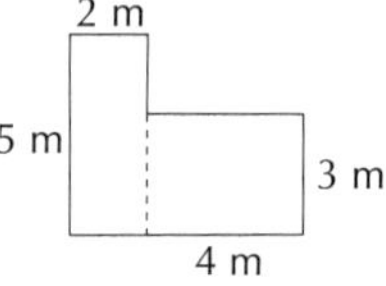

$2 \times 5 = 10$ and $4 \times 3 = 12$, so the total lawn area is $10 + 12 = 22$ m^2. 50 pence = £0.5. So Harvey earns $22 \times 0.5 = £11.00$.

14.   45.5

10% of 70 is 7, so 60% = $7 \times 6 = 42$ and 5% = $7 \div 2 = 3.5$. 65% of 70 = $42 + 3.5 = 45.5$ pages.

15.   E

$a = 2$, so the first term is $3 + 2a = 3 + 2 \times 2 = 3 + 4 = 7$, the second term is $6 + 4 \times 2 = 6 + 8 = 14$, the third term is $9 + 6 \times 2 = 9 + 12 = 21$, and the fourth term is $12 + 8 \times 2 = 12 + 16 = 28$. So the sequence is just the seven times table. The sixth number in the sequence is 42.

Workout 12 — pages 46-48

1. flying
The words can be rearranged into the sentence
'I really want to travel all over the world.'

2. smiles
The words can be rearranged into the sentence
'Playing with my school friends makes me happy.'

3. save
The words can be rearranged into the sentence
'Nobody ate those cupcakes that I made for the party.'

4. vanished
The words can be rearranged into the sentence
'Their camouflage helped to make the soldiers invisible.'

5. excel
The words can be rearranged into the sentence
'The ballerina could not perform her dance routine.'

6. ravine
The other three are areas of raised earth.

7. knot
The other three are electrical cords.

8. dip
The other three mean 'to spread something over an area'.

9. snatch
The other three mean 'to fix in place'.

10. crime
The other three are people who might appear in a courtroom.

11. apprentice
The other three are qualified tradespeople.

12. worsen
'ameliorate' means 'to make better', whereas
'worsen' means 'to make worse'.

13. abhor
'love' means 'to care about deeply', whereas
'abhor' means 'to hate'.

14. energetic
'sluggish' means 'inactive', whereas 'energetic' means 'active'.

15. abundance
'scarcity' means 'shortage', whereas
'abundance' means 'plenty'.

16. durable
'delicate' means 'fragile', whereas 'durable' means 'tough'.

17. believer
'sceptic' means 'someone who doubts something', whereas
'believer' means 'someone who has faith in something'.

18. C
Options A and B have the wrong shading.
Option D is a 90 degree clockwise rotation.

19. B
In option A, the grey rectangle is in the wrong place.
In option C, the white rectangles are in the wrong
places. Option D is a 180 degree rotation.

20. D
Option A has the wrong layering. In option B, the
pentagon and the lower triangle have the wrong
shading. In option C, the triangle has been rotated.

21. D
In option A, the hatching hasn't been reflected. In option B,
the rectangle is in the wrong position. In option C, only
the hatching in the part-circle has been reflected.

22. A
In option B, the square at the bottom is in the wrong place.
In option C, both squares are in the wrong place.
In option D, the square at the top is in the wrong place.

23. B
In option A, the horizontal rectangle is in the wrong
place. In option C, the sloping rectangles have the
wrong hatching. Option D has the wrong layering.

24. C
Options A and D are the wrong shape. Option B
is a 90 degree anticlockwise rotation.

Workout 13 — pages 49-51

1. D
In option D, $33 - 22 = 11$. All the other options equal 12.

2. £21.45
Sebastian finds £5 so adding this to his original
£23.73 gives £28.73. Then subtract the money
he spends on lunch: $28.73 - 7.28 = £21.45$.

3. 1250 m
After 5 minutes Jade has run 750 m and after
9 minutes Jade has run 2000 m. So in the last
four minutes she ran $2000 - 750 = 1250$ m.

4. 45 minutes
2000 m is 2 km. 5×2 km = 10 km, so it will take her
$5 \times 9 = 45$ minutes to run 10 km at that pace.

5. D
Convert all the volumes in litres to pints by dividing by 0.6:
$18 \div 6 = 3$, so $1.8 \div 0.6 = 3$, so Kat drank 3 pints.
$24 \div 6 = 4$, so $2.4 \div 0.6 = 4$, so Justin drank 4 pints.
4 pints is the largest volume so Justin drank the most.

6. 4
Dividing by $^1/_8$ is the same as multiplying by 8. $^1/_2 \times 8 = 4$.

7. 135°
The angles in a triangle add up to 180°, so the two unknown
angles in the triangle add up to $180 - 90 = 90°$.
The two angles are both identical as the triangle is isosceles,
so each one is $90 \div 2 = 45°$. Angles on a straight line
add up to 180°, so the size of y is $180 - 45 = 135°$.

8. record
'record' can mean 'to film' or 'to write down'.

9. round
'round' can mean 'a circular object' or 'one part of a process'.

10. thread
'thread' can mean 'to move between' or 'a piece of string'.

11. grave
'grave' can mean 'significant' or 'without cheer'.

12. toll
'toll' can mean 'a payable charge' or 'a recorded number'.

13. falter
'falter' can mean 'to hesitate' or 'to speak haltingly'.

14. tumultuous
Both words mean 'extremely loud'.

15. determine
Both words mean 'to decide'.

16. radiant
Both words mean 'shining'.

17. raze
Both words mean 'destroy'.

18. heinous
Both words mean 'evil'.

19. unrest
Both words mean 'a state of disturbance'.

Puzzles 5 — page 52

A Sneaky Spider
Outfit D is most like the dress code. Webby's outfit must have four legs with black feet and four legs with white feet. Two legs from each group of four must be solid and the other two must be dashed. There must be four black eyes and four white eyes. The order of shading of the stripes in the oval must match the dress code exactly.

Cube Conundrum
There are 8 cubes with 3 faces painted, 48 cubes with a total of 1 face painted and 8 cubes with no paint on.

Workout 14 — pages 53-56

1. D
Option A is ruled out because the L-shape and the star must be on opposite sides. Option B is ruled out because the triangle and the hourglass shape must be on opposite sides. Option C is ruled out because there is no white semicircle on the net.

2. D
Option A is ruled out because if the two triangles are on the front, and the ring shape is on the top, then the star should be on the left. Option B is ruled out because the wave shape has been rotated. Option C is ruled out because the star and the dots must be on opposite sides.

3. C
Option A is ruled out because if the cross is on the top and the star is on the right, then the circle with the square inside it should be at the back. Option B is ruled out because the two black rectangles and the star must be on opposite sides. Option D is ruled out because the white rectangle has been rotated.

4. A
The bug's eyes and body swap shadings.

5. C
The shading of the bug's head and upper body moves down one place. The shading of the lower body moves to the head. The shading of the bug's feet changes to match the shading of the bug's head.

6. D
The bug's head moves to the front. The bug gains shapes at the ends of its antennae that match the shape of its body. The shading of the bug's body stays the same.

7. C
In each series square, the stars move anticlockwise around the corners.

8. D
In each series square, the number of sides on the shapes increases by one. The number of shapes decreases by one.

9. B
The squares in this series are in two pairs. In each pair, the arrow rotates 45 degrees anticlockwise. The shapes each rotate 90 degrees anticlockwise and swap shading.

10. B
In each series square, the shape at the front and top of the figure moves to the bottom and back of the figure. The hatching moves down one shape.

11. A
In each series square, the rings rotate 90 degrees clockwise. The oval rotates 90 degrees clockwise and moves anticlockwise around the corners of the series square.

12. B
You're looking for the option where 7 is closest to where the decimal point would be.
This is B, where 7 is in the tens column.

13. 7 miles
21 miles ÷ 3 hours = 7 miles per hour.

14. 10
Drawing on the five lines of symmetry gives:

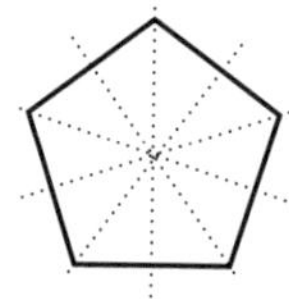

So the pentagon is split into 10 equal pieces.

15. 75 m
8 steps are 200 cm, so each step is
200 ÷ 8 = 25 cm, which is $^1/_4$ m. So 300 steps will be
$^1/_4 \times 300$ m tall. You can use partitioning: $3 \times 100 = 300$,
$^1/_4 \times 100 = 25$, $3 \times 25 = 75$, so $^1/_4 \times 300 = 75$ m.

16. C
10% of 20 = 2, so 60% of 20 = 6 × 2 = 12. So Carlo ran 20 + 12 = 32 km. 8 km goes into 32 km four times, so Carlo ran 4 × 5 = 20 miles and option C is correct.

Workout 15 — pages 57-60

1. D
"loitering" can mean 'walking slowly and aimlessly'.

2. C
Line 5 states that there are "black" tree stumps in the clearing, which suggests that the trees have been burnt. Line 6 states that the clearing contains "the old wreck of forest fires", which shows it has been damaged by fire.

3. D
"bleak" and 'desolate' can both mean 'barren'.

4. A
In lines 11-13, the narrator states that the plants seem like "some spare company / Of hermit folk". "company" means 'a group of people', while "folk" means 'people'.

10

5. B
Here, "chanced upon" means 'came across by accident',
and "way" means 'route taken by a traveller'. "lonely way"
suggests that the path is in a quiet, secluded place.

6. D
Line 20 mentions "the wind's secret stir", which describes
the sound of the wind. Line 30 mentions "dead goldenrod",
which are dead plants. Lines 26-27 state that "The sun
shone out" from a "furrow in the sky" which describes a ray of
sunlight breaking through the clouds. There is no mention of
birds singing.

7. C
Line 32 states that there are "fallen leaves" on the
forest floor that have been "lit" by the sun — these
dead, sunlit leaves are the "rustling yellow multitude".

8. C
In all figures, there should be a trapezium, a
triangle, a diamond and a semicircle.

9. E
In all figures, the number of dots must add up to six.

10. B
In all figures, the number of shapes above the line must
be the same as the number of shapes on the line.

11. A
The figure has been rotated 90 degrees clockwise. In option
B, the figure has been rotated 90 degrees clockwise, then
reflected horizontally. In option C, the line is solid instead
of dashed. In option D, the star is black instead of grey.

12. B
The figure has been rotated 180 degrees. In option A, one
of the dots is in the wrong position. In option C, the figure
has been reflected horizontally. In option D, the figure has
been rotated 180 degrees, then reflected horizontally.

13. C
The figure has been rotated 90 degrees clockwise.
In option A, the figure has been reflected horizontally.
In option B, only the dashed line has been rotated.
In option D, the figure has been rotated 90 degrees
anticlockwise, then reflected vertically.

14. B
The figure has been rotated 180 degrees clockwise.
In option A, the figure has been reflected horizontally.
In option C, the teardrop is at wrong orientation.
In option D, the black shape is at the wrong orientation.

Workout 16 — pages 61-63

1. IV
$24 \div 6 = 4$, which is written IV in Roman numerals.

2. 240 cm³
The volume of the cuboid $= 4 \times 5 \times 12 = 4 \times 60 = 240$ cm³.

3. B
The total amount Amelia earned is $23 \times £41$.
You can use long multiplication to do 23×41:

```
      4 1
   ×  2 3
   -------
    1 2 3
    8 2 0
   -------
  £ 9 4 3
```

4. E
Put $x = 3$ into the expression $x^2 + 3x$: $3^2 + 3 \times 3$.
$3^2 = 9$ and $3 \times 3 = 9$. $9 + 9 = 18$, so option B is correct.

5. 120
The black section is 90° which is $^1/_4$ of the pie chart.
This means the number of people that skied black runs is
$^1/_4 \times 320 = 80$ people.
So the number of people that skied blue runs is
$320 - (20 + 100 + 80) = 320 - 200 = 120$ people.

6. territory
The other three are types of habitat.

7. linger
The other three describe the way that a horse moves.

8. empowered
The other three mean 'showing strong interest'.

9. interval
The other three describe long periods of time.

10. longer
The other three describe the position of
something in relation to something else.

11. sated
'famished' means 'very hungry', whereas 'sated' means 'full'.

12. industrious
'idle' means 'lazy', whereas 'industrious' means 'hard-working'.

13. barbaric
'civilised' means 'sophisticated', whereas
'barbaric' means 'uncivilised'.

14. entwine
'untangle' means 'to untwist', whereas
'entwine' means 'to twist together'.

15. verity
'falsehood' means 'something that is false',
whereas 'verity' means 'truth'.

16. disgrace
'honour' means 'a state of respect', whereas
'disgrace' means 'a state of shame'.

17. convene
'disperse' means 'to move apart', whereas
'convene' means 'to come together'.

18. mesmerise
Both words mean 'capture someone's attention'.

19. silhouette
Both words are lines drawn around an
object to show its shape.

20. doubtful
Both words mean 'uncertain'.

21. negligible
Both words mean 'not important'.

22. haggle
Both words mean 'discuss the terms of a sale'.

23. animated
Both words mean 'lively'.

24. multitude
Both words mean 'a very large amount of something'.

11

Puzzles 6 — page 64

Wobbly Words
risk **rise** rose **lose** lost **list** gist
brave **crave crane** crone **clone alone** along
deceit **decent** recent repent **repeat repeal** reveal

Combination Calculation
1st number: $2 \times 3 = 6$
2nd number: $90 \div 30 = 3$
3rd number: $\frac{3}{5} + \frac{14}{10} = \frac{6}{10} + \frac{14}{10} = \frac{20}{10} = 2$
4th number: $8 - (3 + 2) = 3$
So the combination is: 6323.

Workout 17 — pages 65-67

1. captivated — 'it has **captivated** people'

2. prosperous — 'a mighty and **prosperous** civilisation'

3. residents — 'its **residents** were believed to have'

4. immoral — 'increasingly **immoral** behaviour.'

5. submerged — 'the gods **submerged** Atlantis'

6. little — 'Very **little** trustworthy evidence'

7. unproven — 'several **unproven** theories'

8. eruption — 'a volcanic **eruption**'

9. catastrophic — 'its **catastrophic** end'

10. speculation — '**speculation** remains rife'

11. D
Orla loses 1 point 4 times, so subtract
4 from her score: $-3 - 4 = -7$.

12. 4
Iris is 8 points ahead of Martha, so the number of
questions needed to catch up is $8 \div 2 = 4$.

13. 32 cm
The perimeter of the net is made up of 8 sides of the
triangular faces. The length of each side is
4 cm, so the perimeter is $8 \times 4 = 32$ cm.

14. 1.0175
5600 is 100 times larger than 56, so
$5698 \div 5600$ must be 100 times smaller than
101.75. To divide by 100 move the decimal
point two places to the left, giving 1.0175.

15. E
Convert both times to minutes: 5 hours is
$5 \times 60 = 300$ mins and 6 hours 40 mins is
$6 \times 60 + 40 = 360 + 40 = 400$ mins. This means the
percentage of the journey completed is $\frac{300}{400} = \frac{3}{4} = 75\%$.

16. B
The cost of going to Spain is
$230 + (7 \times 50) = 230 + 350 = £580$.
The cost of going to Greece is
$320 + (7 \times 30) = 320 + 210 = £530$.
The difference in total price is $580 - 530 = £50$.

17. 700 cm²
The width of the frame is $40 + 5 + 5 = 50$ cm.
The height of the frame is $20 + 5 + 5 = 30$ cm.
The total area of the frame is $50 \times 30 = 1500$ cm².
The inner unshaded area is $40 \times 20 = 800$ cm². So the
area of the shaded border is $1500 - 800 = 700$ cm².

Workout 18 — pages 68-71

1. D
Going in a clockwise direction, dashes are added
to the next side of the hexagon. The number of
dashes added increases by one each time.

2. C
The hexagons on opposite sides of the
hexagonal grid are identical.

3. B
Each hexagon is reflected over the line
joining it to the next hexagon.

4. A
Going in a clockwise direction, the inner line in
each hexagon becomes the outer line in the next
hexagon. The keyhole shape rotates 60 degrees.

5. C
Option A is ruled out because the triangle and squares
must be on opposite sides. Option B is ruled out because
the heart and diamond must be on opposite sides. Option
D is ruled out because there is no white triangle on the net.

6. D
Option A is ruled out because if the spiral is at the front
and the semicircle is on the top, then the watch should
be on the left. Option B is ruled out because if the black
triangles are at the front and the hexagon is on the top,
then the pencil should be on the left. Option C is ruled out
because there is only one set of black triangles on the net.

7. C
Option A is ruled out because the shape on the
right isn't on the net. Option B is ruled out because
the leaf shape and the lightning bolt should be on
opposite sides. Option D is ruled out because the
face with the circle and lines has been rotated.

8. C
Option A is ruled out because the black square and white
teardrop has been rotated. Option B is ruled out because
if the circle and lines are at the front and the cloud shape
is on the top, then the arrow should be on the left. Option
D is ruled out because one of the arrow heads is incorrect.

9. B
Option A is ruled out because the circles and line have been
rotated. Option C is ruled out because the face with the
star has the wrong shading. Option D is ruled out because
if the shield is at the front and the circles and line are
on the top, then the semicircles should be on the left.

10. D
Option A is ruled out because the part circle and star
have been rotated. Option B is ruled out because the star
is missing on the right-hand face. Option C is ruled out
because if the three arrow shapes are on the front and the
triangle is on the top, then the five lines should be on the left.

11. B
Option A is ruled out because the shaded rectangles have been rotated. Option C is ruled out because the shading of the rectangles is wrong. Option D is ruled out because if the semicircles are at the front and the black square is on the top, then the hexagons should be on the left.

12. learnt
The words can be rearranged into the sentence 'The pilot loved teaching people how to fly planes.'

13. growth
The words can be rearranged into the sentence 'Oak trees can live for over one thousand years.'

14. saved
The words can be rearranged into the sentence 'Hamsters can store lots of food in their cheek pouches.'

15. crown
The words can be rearranged into the sentence 'Many English swans belong to Her Majesty the Queen.'

16. must
The words can be rearranged into the sentence 'There was no way anyone could have prepared for this.'

17. crime
The words can be rearranged into the sentence 'Mark's testimony helped the police to catch a burglar.'

18. dull
'dull' can mean 'boring' or 'lacking colour'.

19. shake
'shake' can mean 'to shudder' or 'to cause distress'.

20. boil
'boil' can mean 'a swelling on the skin' or 'to bubble'.

21. bear
'bear' can mean 'to transport' or 'to hold the weight of'.

22. basin
'basin' can mean 'a hollow in land' or 'a container'.

23. cloak
'cloak' can mean 'to hide something' or 'a sleeveless item of clothing worn on the shoulders'.

Workout 19 — pages 72-75

1. A
The top block in A goes at the right of the figure at the back. The other two blocks in A are arranged to the left and in front of it.

2. D
The bottom block in D goes at the back of the figure. The middle block in D goes on top of it. The top two blocks in D go at the front of the figure.

3. C
The top block in C goes at the back of the figure on the top. The other two blocks in C are arranged in front of and below it.

4. D
Shape D has been rotated 90 degrees left-to-right.

5. E
Shape E has been rotated 90 degrees clockwise in the plane of the page.

6. A
Shape A has been rotated 90 degrees left-to-right.

7. C
Shape C has been rotated 90 degrees right-to-left. It has then been rotated 90 degrees away from you, top-to-bottom.

8. 3450 ml
There are 1000 millilitres in a litre, so $3.45 \times 1000 = 3450$ ml.

9. A
Options C, D and E are all too small because x is a reflex angle. Option B is too large as x is only slightly wider than a straight line (180 °). So option A must be correct.

10. 288
1% of 800 is 8, so 36% of 800 is 8×36. Using partitioning $8 \times 36 = 240 + 48 = 288$.

11. Day 6
On Day 4 the tree will have $24 \div 2 = 12$ leaves left, on Day 5 it will have $12 \div 2 = 6$ leaves left and on Day 6 it will have $6 \div 2 = 3$ leaves left, which is an odd number.

12. E
The total number of items is $15 + 8 + 4 = 27$. $^{15}/_{27}$ are plastic, which is equivalent to $^{5}/_{9}$.

13. E
Cycling 12 mph means it take one hour to cycle 12 miles. So to cycle 8 miles, it'll take $^{8}/_{12}$ of an hour. $^{1}/_{12}$ of an hour is 5 minutes, so $^{8}/_{12}$ is $5 \times 8 = 40$ minutes.

14. C
The base of each triangle is the radius of the circle, which is half the diameter: $4a \div 2 = 2a$. The area of one triangle is $^{1}/_{2} \times 2a \times 2b = a \times 2b = 2ab$. There are four fan blades so the total area is $4 \times 2ab = 8ab$.

Workout 20 — pages 76-79

1. C
Line 2 states that the housing estate has existed for "less than a decade", so it can't be more than ten years old. This means that the housing estate was built after the "hundred-year-old well" (line 1).

2. B
Line 2 states that "Stones were missing" from the well. 'Dilapidated' means 'falling apart'.

3. B
'sceptical' means 'doubtful'. Line 9 states that Chris "scoffed that the monsters were far too clever to be caught". This suggests he doubts that Alice's plan to find proof of a monster will be successful.

4. C
Line 11 states that locals "complained" that the well was "a hazard", which suggests that the council put a grate over the top to make it less dangerous.

5. A
Line 15 states that Alice hopes she might find "remnants" of a monster visit, which would prove a monster had been at the well.

6. D
Line 18 states that the torch falls with "a resounding clatter", which shows it makes a lot of noise.

7.   C
Line 19 states that "Alice's heart was pounding" and
"She took a step back", which suggests she is alarmed.

8.   C
All figures must be identical apart from rotation.

9.   C
All figures must be made up of two identical,
overlapping shapes with the same shading.
The overlapping area must have different shading.

10.   D
All figures must have two sets of two identical shapes.
The shading of the shapes in each set must be the same.

11.   D
In all figures the circles must decrease in size along
the line. The shading of the circles must alternate.

12.   E
In all figures, there must be three circles inside the large
shape. The number of lines around the outside of the large
shape must be half the number of sides of the large shape.

13.   B
In all figures, the order of white shapes front-to-back must
be the same as the order of black shapes bottom-to-top.

14.   B
All figures must contain the same number
of parallel lines as points on the star.

Puzzles 7 — page 80

Typo Trouble
The correct words are: **major, abject, torment,
hearth, accent, irate, chatter, mature**

Mirror, Mirror...
D

Workout 21 — pages 81-83

1.   180 000
You're rounding to the nearest thousand so you have
to look at the digit in the hundreds column. It's 5, so
you round the thousands digit up to give 180 000.

2.   131°
Angles on a straight line add up to 180:
$x = 180 - 49 = 131°$.

3.   15
Sparrows made the most visits with 19, and wrens made
the fewest with 4. The difference is $19 - 4 = 15$.

4.   D
18 out of the 72 visits were made by blackbirds.
$^{18}/_{72} = ^{9}/_{36} = ^{1}/_{4}$. $^{1}/_{4}$ of a circle is 90°.

5.   D
First count forwards 8 hours to get 01:25. Then add on
40 minutes to get 02:05, which is shown in option D.

6.   4
To calculate the mean number of fish per hour you need to
divide the total number Nico caught by the time he spent
fishing in hours. Nico caught a total of $5 + 3 + 2 = 10$ fish.
You know that $100 ÷ 25 = 4$, so $10 ÷ 2.5$ is also 4.

7.   E
Put b into the equation: $4a + (3 \times -12) = 4a - 36 = -24$.
If you subtract 36 from a number and get -24, then you
must've started with 12: so $4a = 12$. $4 \times 3 = 12$, so $a = 3$.

8.   overwhelmingly — '**overwhelmingly** popular'

9.   Traditional — '**Traditional** pizza originates from'

10.   nourishing — 'a cheap and **nourishing** meal.'

11.   seafarers — 'which was eaten by **seafarers**'

12.   allegedly — 'which was **allegedly** named after'

13.   evoke — 'are said to **evoke**'

14.   across — 'increasingly popular **across** America'

15.   independent — 'their own **independent** pizzerias.'

16.   authentic — 'an **authentic** Neapolitan pizza'

17.   kneaded — 'must have been **kneaded** by hand'

Workout 22 — pages 84-86

1.   D
Option A is a 90 degree clockwise rotation.
Option B has the wrong shading. In option C,
the heart shape hasn't been reflected.

2.   C
Options A and D are the wrong shape.
Option B is a 90 degree anticlockwise rotation.

3.   A
In option B, the black triangle is in the wrong place.
Option C has the wrong layering.
Option D is a 45 degree clockwise rotation.

4.   D
In option A, the moon shapes haven't been reflected.
Option B is a 180 degree rotation.
In option C, the stars have swapped places.

5.   D
Option A is the wrong shape. In option B, the largest
shape hasn't been reflected. In option C, the black
and white stripes haven't been reflected.

6.   E
All figures must have a black shape behind a shape with
hatching. The hatched shape must be to the top right
of the black shape. The shapes cannot be the same.

7.   B
All figures must have a row of three identical shapes that
alternate between grey and white shading. The two outer
shapes must contain a smaller, grey version of the shape.

8.   C
All figures must contain two identical large shapes.
The large shapes must contain smaller shapes
that are downward reflections of each other.

9.   D
All figures must contain a black shape that is
surrounded by the same number of lines as its
number of sides. One of the lines must be dashed.

10.   D
In all figures, the cross must have the same shading
as the large shape. The cross must be behind
the line. The line must extend out of the large shape.

11. A
All figures must contain half the number of
black circles as there are white circles.

12. 26
The ratio of pigs to sheep is 2 : 3. Sheep make up 3 parts of
the ratio, so divide 39 by 3: 39 ÷ 3 = 13. Pigs make up two
parts of the ratio so multiply 13 by 2: 13 × 2 = 26 pigs.

13. 31.5 cm³
The volume of the matchbox is 2 × 4.5 × 3.5. 2 × 4.5 = 9
and 9 × 3.5 = 31.5 cm³ (you can use partitioning here).

14. D
Work out the price of each of the salads from the
graph: 2 extras = £7, 3 extras = £8.50, 5 extras
= £11.50. The total is 7 + 8.5 + 11.5 = £27.

15. £14.50
Put 7 into the formula: P = 4 + (1.5 × 7).
You can use partioning here: 1.5 = 1 + 0.5.
1 × 7 = 7 and 0.5 × 7 = 3.5, so 1.5 × 7 = 7 + 3.5 = 10.5.
This means P = 4 + 10.5 = £14.50.

Workout 23 — pages 87-90

1. A
The white shape has a section cut from it in the shape of
the black shape. The shading of the shape becomes grey.

2. C
The two shapes swap positions and outlines. The black
shape becomes white and the arrow is rotated 180 degrees.

3. D
The shape is reflected downwards and combines with
its reflection. The hatching of the reflected part is
rotated 90 degrees. The combined shape is rotated 90
degrees clockwise and the hatching swaps shading.

4. B
There are five blocks visible from above, which rules
out options A and D. There is one block visible on
the right-hand side, which rules out option C.

5. A
There are six blocks visible from above, which
rules out options C and D. There are three blocks
visible at the back, which rules out option B.

6. B
There are three blocks visible on the left-hand side,
which rules out options C and D. There are two blocks
visible at the back, which rules out option A.

7. B
There are six blocks visible from above, which rules
out option A. There are two blocks visible on the
left-hand side, which rules out option D. There are two
blocks visible at the back, which rules out option C.

8. A
Working from top to bottom, a new, identical shape is
added on top of the previous shape. The second shape
added is black and the third shape added is grey.

9. C
Working from left to right, the figure rotates
45 degrees anticlockwise and changes
shading from white, to grey, to black.

10. B
Working from top to bottom, the figure in the first grid
square and the figure in the second grid square are added
together to make the figure in the third grid square.

11. A
Working from left to right, each dot moves one place
clockwise around the edge of the grid square.

12. foreign
Both words mean 'unknown'.

13. cantankerous
Both words mean 'irritable'.

14. fume
Both words mean 'to feel great anger'.

15. vindictive
Both words mean 'acting out of a desire for revenge'.

16. deviation
Both words mean 'a departure from a set course'.

17. confirm
'deny' means 'to dispute the truth of something', whereas
'confirm' means 'to state that something is true'.

18. retract
'extend' can mean 'hold out', whereas
'retract' means 'to draw back'.

19. bias
'disinterest' means 'lack of prejudice', whereas 'bias'
means 'prejudice for or against something'.

20. flawless
'blemished' means 'flawed', whereas 'flawless' means 'perfect'.

21. disassemble
'construct' means 'build', whereas
'disassemble' means 'take apart'.

22. collect
'distribute' means 'give out', whereas
'collect' means 'gather in'.

23. confidently
'uncertainly' means 'hesitantly', whereas
'confidently' means 'with certainty'.

Puzzles 8 — page 91

Loopy Snooker
80°

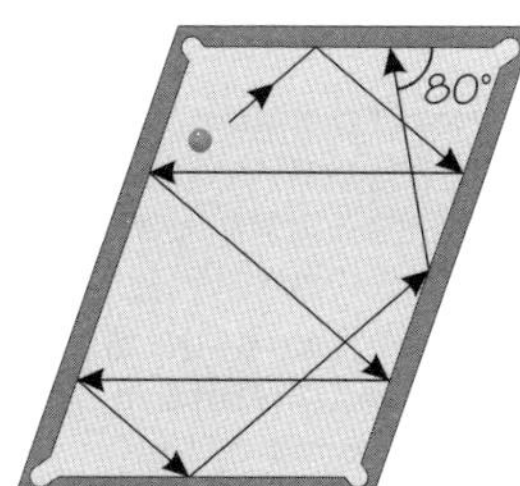

Hexagonal Havoc
Gap 1 — tile A
Gap 2 — tile C
Gap 3 — tile F
Gap 4 — tile H

Workout 24 — pages 92-95

1.   E
Put the wingspans in order from largest to smallest:
1.12 m, 102 cm, 0.85 cm, 73 cm, 71 cm, 65 cm, 0.5 m.
The fourth largest is 73 cm.

2.   62 cm
Convert the largest and smallest wingspan to cm:
112 cm and 50 cm. The difference between
the wingspans is 112 − 50 = 62 cm.

3.   14 left and 2 up
Pick a corner of the shaded rectangle and work out
how far it needs to move to get to the dotted rectangle
— it needs to move 14 units to the left and 2 units up.

4.   0.2
$8 \div 4 = 2$ and 0.8 is ten times smaller
than 8, so $0.8 \div 4 = 0.2$.

5.   4.5 m²
Work out the area of carpet needed for each room.
$2.5 \times 4 = 10$ m² and $3 \times 3.5 = 10.5$ m² (you can use
partitioning here). In total Bryony will use
$10.5 + 10 = 20.5$ m² for the two rooms. The area
of carpet she will have left is 25 − 20.5 m = 4.5 m².

6.   A
The amount Lesley earns increases by 3 every day, so the
n^{th} term must include $3n$. This means it cannot be option
B, or C. It also cannot be option D because it describes
a decreasing sequence. It also cannot be option E,
because it doesn't match the sequence, e.g. $n = 1$ would
give $3 \times 1 + 1 = 4$. So the answer must be option A.

7.   D
If a $^1/_4$ of the cheese weighs 16 g the entire cube
must weigh $4 \times 16 = 64$ g. 1 cm³ weighs 1 g so the
cube has a volume of 64 cm³. You're looking for the
height option that would give a volume of 64 cm³.
Only option D, $4 \times 4 \times 4$, gives 64, so the answer is 4 cm.

8.   B
The bottom block in B goes at the back of
the figure. The other two blocks in B are
arranged on top of and in front of it.

9.   B
The bottom left block in B goes at the back of the
figure on the left. The top block in B is arranged
on top of and to the right of it. The bottom right
block in B goes at the front of the figure.

10.   D
The middle block in D goes at the back of the figure on the
right. The top two blocks in D are arranged to the left of
it. The bottom block in D goes at the front of the figure.

11.   C
The top block in C is rotated 90 degrees right-to-left and
goes at the back of the figure on the right. The bottom
right block in C is arranged below it. The remaining two
blocks in C are arranged on the left of the figure.

12.   A
The top right block in A goes at the back of the figure.
The bottom two blocks in A are arranged in front of it.
The top left block in A goes at the front of the figure.

13.   D
The bottom left block in D goes at the back of the figure on
the left. The top block in D goes on top of and to the right of
it. The bottom right block in D goes at the front of the figure.

14.   B
The middle block in B goes at the back of the figure
on the left. The top block and bottom right block
in B are arranged in front of it. The bottom left
block in B goes at the front of the figure.

Workout 25 — pages 96-98

1.   dedicated
Both words mean 'devoted'.

2.   mourn
Both words mean 'to express sorrow'.

3.   revelation
Both words can mean 'something that has been made known'.

4.   obstinate
Both words mean 'determined not to change'.

5.   anticipate
Both words mean 'to guess what will happen'.

6.   lap
'lap' can mean 'a complete run of a racing circuit' or 'to slosh'.

7.   tough
'tough' can mean 'durable' or 'challenging'.

8.   level
'level' can mean 'destroy' or 'status'.

9.   tip
'tip' can mean 'the uppermost point of
something' or 'to overbalance'.

10.   volume
'volume' can mean 'the amount of space
something takes up' or 'one book in a series'.

11.   9
$5^2 - 4^2 = 5 \times 5 - 4 \times 4 = 25 - 16 = 9$.

12.   C
The ratio of sugar to flour is 60 grams : 180 grams.
Dividing each side of the ratio by 60 gives $60 \div 60 = 1$
and $180 \div 60 = 3$. So the ratio is 1:3.

13.   B
$^3/_8$ is the same as $^6/_{16}$, so $^3/_{16} + ^3/_8 = ^3/_{16} + ^6/_{16} = ^9/_{16}$.

14.   70
The height of the rectangles increases by 1 each time and
the width increases by 2 each time. The next rectangle
in the sequence will have a height of $6 + 1 = 7$ and a
width of $8 + 2 = 10$. So the area is $7 \times 10 = 70$.

15.   D
From a plan view
only the top faces
can be seen, so D
shows the correct shape.

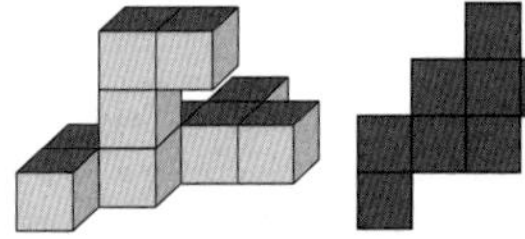

16.   2
$32 \div 4 = 8$, so you know that $2a = 4$. $2 \times 2 = 4$, so $a = 2$.

17.   1800 m

£45 isn't shown on the graph. But 45 = 3 × 15,
so read off £15 the graph — this is 3.5 km:

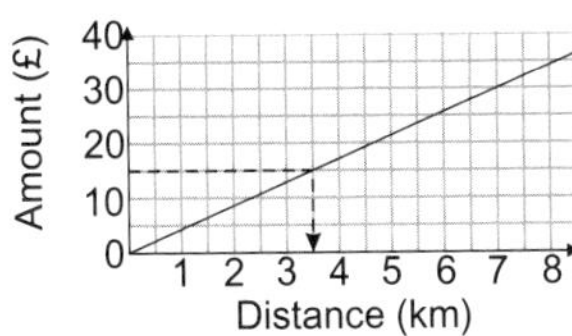

So Ivan ran 3 × 3.5 = 10.5 km (you can use
partitioning here). Karina ran 12.3 – 10.5 = 1.8 km
further, which is 1800 m.

Workout 26 — pages 99-101

1.   B
All other figures contain only two types of shading.

2.   E
All other figures contain a shape with six sides.

3.   C
In all other figures, the shading changes
along a line of symmetry.

4.   B
All other figures contain a black circle
inside the large white shape.

5.   B
All other figures contain arrows with
heads that match the large shape.

6.   D
In all other figures, the arrow points towards the
circle that is the only one with its shading.

7.   E
In all other figures, the grey shape in the middle can be
rotated and enlarged to complete the white shape.

8.   weak
The words can be rearranged into the sentence
'Her letter to the paper was incredibly well written.'

9.   mask
The words can be rearranged into the sentence
'Everyone on the building site promised to wear helmets.'

10.   sirens
The words can be rearranged into the sentence
'My alarm clock isn't loud enough to wake me up.'

11.   failure
The words can be rearranged into the sentence
'Katie's dad climbed Mount Everest when he was younger.'

12.   smelled
The words can be rearranged into the sentence
'Our new pet mouse does not like to eat cheese.'

13.   lithe
The other three mean 'smooth'.

14.   stutter
The other three mean 'to move haltingly'.

15.   spectacles
The other three are worn on the wrist.

16.   recall
The other three mean 'to move away from somewhere'.

17.   flush
The other three are used to describe deep lines in something.

18.   alternate
The other three all mean 'to turn'.

19.   severe
'lenient' means 'merciful', whereas 'severe' means 'harsh'.

20.   harmless
'noxious' means 'harmful', whereas
'harmless' means 'doesn't cause harm'.

21.   ascend
'plunge' means 'to drop down', whereas
'ascend' means 'to go up'.

22.   humility
'pride' means 'arrogance', whereas 'humility'
means 'having a modest opinion of yourself'.

23.   superficial
'deep' can mean 'beyond the surface', whereas
'superficial' can mean 'only on the surface'.

24.   unauthorised
'official' means 'approved', whereas
'unauthorised' means 'not approved'.

25.   improvement
'deterioration' means 'the worsening of something', whereas
'improvement' means 'the betterment of something'.

Puzzles 9 — page 102

Superior Synonyms
The synonyms are: affable, convinced,
ferocious, intimidates, gigantic, cunning

Mind the Cliff
3 blasts of the burner and dropping 3 ballasts will cause the
balloon the rise 60 m: (3 × 13) + (3 × 7) = 39 + 21 = 60 m.

Amanda must use the burner 5 times:
The balloon will travel forwards 5 × 9 = 45 m and rise
5 × 13 = 65 m, clearing the height of the cliff.

Workout 27 — pages 103-106

1.   C
Line 3 states that the Brontës lived in an "impoverished
village". 'deprived' and 'impoverished' both mean 'poor'.

2.   B
Lines 5-6 state that "as children" the Brontës created
"elaborate fantasy worlds". Line 8 states that "This
sparked their ambition to become published authors".

3.   C
Lines 11-12 state that the Brontës published under
"names that disguised their female identity", one
of which was "Acton Bell". Lines 12-13 state that
these names "corresponded to the initials of their real
names", so "Acton Bell" must refer to Anne Brontë.

4. C
Lines 13-14 state that "people considered it inappropriate for women to make a living from writing", which made the Brontës fear they'd "face prejudice" (line 15). This suggests that they were worried about being refused by publishers because of their gender.

5. A
Line 16 states that the Brontës' "poetry only sold a handful of copies", which shows that it didn't sell well.

6. D
Lines 19-21 state that people were shocked by the "cruelty and violence" in 'Wuthering Heights' and the "harrowing themes" in 'The Tenant of Wildfell Hall'. "harrowing" means 'very distressing'.

7. D
Line 22 states that the Brontë sisters are "renowned for their contribution to literature", which shows that their work is still influential.

8. 4
Eleanor will receive £4.20 change. £4 of her change is given as coins so 20p is given in 5 pence pieces. So the number of 5 pence pieces she receives is $20 \div 5 = 4$.

9. 9 cm
Gerry has 4 cm left so he used $85 - 4 = 81$ cm. The length of the 9 pieces he cut is $81 \div 9 = 9$ cm.

10. B
The lake fully covers approximately 13 squares and covers more than half of 5 squares. So the area is estimated as $13 + 5 = 18$ km^2.

11. E
Option D is the only expression which is not true, because $160 - 79 = 81$ and $41 \times 2 = 82$.

12. €302
Nestor rented the car for 5 days so $d = 5$. Put d into the expression: $30 \times 5 + 2m = 150 + 2m$. m, the number of miles Nestor drove over 500 is $576 - 500 = 76$. Put m into the expression: $150 + 2 \times 76 = 150 + 152 = €302$.

Workout 28 — pages 107-110

1. B
The number of chocolates Victor needs to eat to have 1 left is $25 - 1 = 24$. He eats three a day so the number of days it will take him to eat 24 is $24 \div 3 = 8$.

2. 40 cm
The depth at the deepest point is the radius of the semicircle. The diameter is 0.8 m which is 80 cm, so the radius is $80 \div 2 = 40$ cm.

3. D
The number of Monday's emails that were not advertising is $25 - 15 = 10$. So the percentage of emails that were not advertising is $^{10}/_{25} = ^{2}/_{5} = 40\%$.

4. 9
There are 5 days in total, so if the mean is 12.2 then the total number of advertising emails Uma received is $5 \times 12.2 = 61$ (you can use partitioning here). The total number of advertising emails Uma received on Monday, Wednesday, Thursday and Friday is $15 + 6 + 10 + 21 = 52$. So the number of advertising emails Uma received on Tuesday is $61 - 52 = 9$.

5. 300°
Donna has gone through $^{4}/_{24} = ^{1}/_{6}$ of the ferris wheel's full rotation. $^{1}/_{6}$ of $360°$ is $360 \div 60 = 60°$, so she has $360 - 60 = 300°$ to go until she is back at the start.

6. B
The figure is rotated 135 degrees anticlockwise. In option A, the star hasn't been rotated. In option C, the star has the wrong shading. In option D, the shape is wrong.

7. C
The figure is rotated 180 degrees. Option A is a rotated reflection. In option B, the black shape is wrong. In option D, the shading of the hexagon is wrong.

8. C
The figure is rotated 90 degrees clockwise. In option A, there is no dashed line. In option B, the hearts have been rotated. Option D is a rotated reflection.

9. D
The figure is rotated 180 degrees. In option A, the triangle is wrong. In option B, the grey part-circle is the wrong shape. In option C, the white arrow is pointing the wrong way.

10. B
The figure is rotated 135 degrees anticlockwise. In option A, the large square is at the wrong orientation. In option C, the arrow is too long. In option D, the arrow is pointing the wrong way.

11. B
All the circles in the bug become squares and all the ovals become rectangles. The bug's legs also straighten.

12. C
The bug's wings split in half and its eyes turn black.

13. C
The shading on the bug's body is reversed. The hatching in the left eye is rotated 45 degrees anticlockwise. The hatching in the right eye is rotated 45 degrees clockwise. The number of legs doubles.

14. C
The whole grid has a vertical line of symmetry.

15. A
Going in a clockwise direction, the black shapes match the shape in the centre hexagon that is next to the previous hexagon.

16. D
Going in a clockwise direction, the shading of the inner arrows changes in the order: black, grey, white. Going in an anticlockwise direction, the shading of the outer arrows changes in the order: black, grey, white.

Workout 29 — pages 111-114

1.   D
Lines 2-3 state that the "large airy sitting-room"
is "illuminated by two broad windows", which
suggests it is roomy and bright.

2.   A
Line 4 states that the "terms" (the cost) for
renting the apartment were "moderate", which
suggests that the rent wasn't too expensive.

3.   B
Line 5 states that "the bargain was concluded upon the
spot", meaning that they quickly decided they wanted the
apartment. 'decisively' means 'quickly and confidently'.

4.   A
Line 12 states that Sherlock's "habits were regular",
showing that he behaves in a similar way every day.
This suggests his movements are easy to predict.

5.   C
'invariably' and 'consistent' both mean 'without change'.

6.   D
Line 14 states that Sherlock spends time in "the chemical
laboratory" and "the dissecting-rooms". These locations
are both associated with scientific study.

7.   C
'intrigued' means 'interested'. In line 20,
John states that he has an "interest in"
Sherlock and "curiosity as to his aims in life".

8.   4691
$0.5 \times 4691 \times 2$ is the same as
$(0.5 \times 2) \times 4691 = 1 \times 4691 = 4691$.

9.   9
Divide the number of brushes by the number each pot can
hold: $91 \div 11 = 8$ remainder 3. So to hold all the brushes,
there needs to be 9 pots.

10.   C
The volume of each well is $2 \times 2 \times 2 = 8 \text{ cm}^3$. There are
12 wells so the total volume is $8 \times 12 = 96 \text{ cm}^3$.

11.   A
The wasp section of the pie chart is 110° and the
bee section is 100°. So work out $110 + 100 = 210$
as a fraction of 360. $\frac{210}{360} = \frac{21}{36} = \frac{7}{12}$.

12.   2
Work out the size of the butterfly section:
$360 - (110 + 100 + 90 + 40) = 360 - 340 = 20°$.
Half of those are white so $20 \div 2 = 10°$ represents
white butterflies. $10°$ is $\frac{1}{36}$ of a circle. $\frac{1}{36}$ of the total
number of insects is $72 \div 36 = 2$ white butterflies.

Workout 30 — pages 115-118

1.   6:50 pm
Harper arrives at 8:25 pm. Taking off an hour
gets 7:25 pm, then taking off 25 minutes gets 7:00 pm.
Taking off the final 10 minutes gives 6:50 pm.

2.   £10
The towel was bought in a 20% sale, so £8 is
80% of the full price. So 10% of the full price is
$£8 \div 8 = £1$. This means the full price is £10.

3.   4206
The greatest number of steps in one day is 12 098
and the fewest is 7892. Use written subtraction:

$$\begin{array}{r} {}^{0}{}^{1}{}^{1}{}^{1}\\ 1\,2\,0\,9\,8 \\ -\quad 7\,8\,9\,2 \\ \hline 4\,2\,0\,6 \end{array}$$

4.   C
The number of steps taken each day are approximately
8000, 12 000, 10 000, 11 000 and 9000.
Use these values to estimate the mean:
$8000 + 12\,000 + 10\,000$
$\qquad + 11\,000 + 9000 = 50\,000$.
Dividing by the number of days
gives $50\,000 \div 5 = 10\,000$.
Option C is the only option close to this value.

5.   E
Rory has completed 4.5 of his target 8 lengths.
The fraction of the target he has completed is $4.5 \div 8$,
which is equivalent to $9 \div 16$, which is the same as $\frac{9}{16}$.

6.   D
The rectangle has a width of 2, so the x-coordinate
of P will be 2 greater than that of P, which is
$b + 2$. The rectangle has a height of 4, so the
y-coordinate of q will be 4 greater than that of p:
$3 + 4 = 7$. So the coordinate of Q is $(b + 2, 7)$.

7.   C
Compare the old and new coordinates of $P(b, 3)$ and
$(-b, 2)$. $-b$ is $2b$ less than b so the rectangle must have
been moved left by $2b$ units. 2 is one less than 3 so the
rectangle must have been moved down by one unit.

8.   B
The arrow points to the shape with
the most lines of symmetry.

9.   D
The figure is reflected vertically.

10.   A
The grey shapes move to the front of the figure and
turn black. The outer shape turns white. A small
grey shape appears in the centre of the figure.

11.   E
Shape E has been rotated 180 degrees
in the plane of the page.

12.   A
Shape A has been rotated 90 degrees
away from you from top-to-bottom.

13.   B
Shape B has been rotated 90 degrees towards
you from top-to-bottom. It has then been rotated
180 degrees in the plane of the page.

14.   D
Shape D has been rotated 90 degrees towards
you from top-to-bottom. It has then been
rotated 90 degrees from right-to-left.

Gently does it... Please remove this Answer Book carefully to keep your books in perfect condition!